GRAND PRIX PREVIEW 99

HAZLETON PUBLISHING

PUBLISHER
RICHARD POULTER

WRITTEN BY
TONY DODGINS

ART EDITOR
MICHAEL WHITMORE

PRODUCTION MANAGER
STEVEN PALMER

PUBLISHING DEVELOPMENT MANAGER
SIMON MAURICE

BUSINESS DEVELOPMENT MANAGER
SIMON SANDERSON

SALES PROMOTION
CLARE KRISTENSEN

PHOTOGRAPHY
LAT PHOTOGRAPHIC

FRONT COVER PHOTOGRAPHY
GIANNI GIANSANTI

GRAND PRIX PREVIEW
is published by
Hazleton Publishing Ltd,
3 Richmond Hill,
Richmond, Surrey
TW10 6RE, England.

Colour reproduction by
Barrett Berkeley Ltd, London, England.

Printed in England by
Jarrold Book Printing, Thetford, Norfolk.

***Contents correct at time of going to press**

ISBN: 1-874557-73X

DISTRIBUTORS

UNITED KINGDOM
Biblios Ltd
Star Road
Partridge Green
West Sussex RH13 8LD
Telephone: 01403 710971
Fax: 01403 711143

NORTH AMERICA
Motorbooks International
PO Box 1
729 Prospect Ave., Osceola
Wisconsin 54020, USA
Telephone: (1) 715 294 3345
Fax: (1) 715 294 4448

AUSTRALIA
Technical Book and
Magazine Co. Pty
295 Swanston Street
Melbourne, Victoria 3000
Telephone: (03) 9663 3951
Fax: (03) 9662 2094

NEW ZEALAND
David Bateman Ltd
P.O. Box 100-242
North Shore Mail Centre
Auckland 1330
Telephone: (9) 415 7664
Fax: (9) 415 8892

SOUTH AFRICA
Motorbooks
341 Jan Smuts Avenue
Craighall Park
Johannesburg
Telephone: (011) 325 4458/60
Fax: (1) 325 4146

Contents

Foreword

The countdown to the start of any new Formula 1 season is always an exciting time. On the face of it, the glitzy car presentations and the many articles speculating on the new season keep the journalists busy and the fans happy. But behind the scenes, all the teams and drivers work hard on and off the track to get their cars ready. We all aim for the same goal: to be competitive at the first Grand Prix, in Australia.

For me, the anticipation of the new season is greater than ever. I am with a brand-new team, British American Racing, and hopes are high for a strong debut on the race track. So far, I am happy with our preparations. Embarking on this new adventure was definitely the right move.

It was clear from the outset that this team is different. The positive spirit at British American Racing is very motivating. I know I can trust the people I work with. They share the same determination to challenge the odds – and win. I enjoy this new atmosphere. It's like a breath of fresh air.

I feel that the final Formula 1 season of this Millennium will prove to be one of the most exciting ever. The competition is likely to be closer and more hard-fought. At British American Racing, we will put our best efforts together to achieve success and make our first season a year to remember.

In any event, I hope this 1999 preview will get you in the starting mood for the on-track battles of the forthcoming season. Personally, I can't wait. See you in Melbourne.

Jacques Villeneuve

TELEGLOBE
LUCKY STRIKE
J. VILLENEUVE
AMERICAN ORIGINAL

Introduction

Formula 1 has come a long way since the days when it was largely a sport for moneyed gentleman racers.

Even as recently as the early eighties it was possible for a team to win the world championship with a relatively inexpensive off-the-shelf customer engine bolted into the back of a custom-built chassis. That led to the current proliferation of specialist British constructors which still dominate the sport. The manufacturer teams, such as Ferrari and Renault — 'the Grandees' — labelled these specialist outfits 'the garagistes'.

Things have changed. Today, major motor manufacturers see Formula 1 as an important tool for raising their image. Since Mercedes became associated with McLaren and the team changed to its silver livery, for example, the sale of silver Mercedes has increased by almost 30 per cent and the average age of the Mercedes buyer has dropped, reflecting a more sporting appeal.

Mercedes took their first championship in 1998 and among the opposition are Ferrari (Fiat), Mugen Honda (Jordan), Peugeot (Prost) and Ford (Stewart). Waiting

in the wings are BMW, which starts a partnership with Williams in 2000, Honda themselves and Toyota. Never has F1's future been rosier.

That, though, is only one part of the story. Formula 1 is really about human drama and never has the public interest been higher. Some claim there is not enough overtaking, but others say the balance is right. FIA president Max Mosley makes the pertinent point that with a basketball game or a motorcycle race, where scored baskets or overtaking moves are commonplace, they lack impact. You can put the kettle on without fear of missing something important.

Not so with Formula 1. Proof that Mosley is right is the number of complaints ITV receives about its advertising breaks from frustrated enthusiasts! Grand Prix racing is full of side issues and rivalries on both the human and technical fronts. The more you know about it, the more enjoyment it will give you. What we have tried to do is provide an insight into the multi faceted world of F1 and help you get the most out of the 1999 season. Happy viewing!

THE TEAMS

Mob

McLAREN

The team's heritage dates back to 1963 when Kiwi Bruce McLaren formed a company to build cars bearing his own name. The first McLaren made its Grand Prix debut at Monte Carlo in 1966 and the marque took its first victory at Spa two years later with Bruce himself driving. Tragically, the popular New Zealander was killed testing an M8 CanAm sportscar at Goodwood on June 2, 1970.

The original orange McLaren livery was first replaced in 1974 when the team entered into a commercial deal with Philip Morris (Marlboro) which resulted in one of the longest sponsorship associations in sporting history. It was finally dissolved at the end of 1995 when McLaren and Reemtsma (West) joined forces.

McLaren International came into being in 1980 when McLaren merged with Ron Dennis's Project Four organisation. Dennis is a stickler for detail and prides himself on a professional approach. Under his leadership the team emerged as the dominant force of the mid eighties, winning consecutive drivers' championships with Niki Lauda and Alain Prost (twice) in 1984-86. In 1988 with Prost and Ayrton Senna, the team won 15 of the season's 16 races!

A barren spell followed the withdrawal of engine supplier Honda in 1992, but not barren enough to stop Senna taking the team to the top of the all-time race winners list ahead of Ferrari by the end of 1993. They started 1999 three behind the Maranello team, with 116 wins. A new partnership with Mercedes-Benz for 1995 put the team back on the right track. The recruitment of design guru Adrian Newey for 1998 helped turn the MP4-13 into a world-beater and put the team back on top. They are the ones to shoot at this year.

McLaren International
Woking Business Park
Albert Drive
Woking
Surrey GU21 5JY
England
Tel: 44 (0) 1483 711311
Fax: 44 (0) 1483 711312

1 Mika Hakkinen (SF)

2 David Coulthard (GB)

MILESTONES
Constructors' championship titles: 1974, '84, '85, '88, '89, '90, '91, '98
Drivers' championship titles: 1974 (Fittipaldi), '76 (Hunt), '84 (Lauda), '85, '86 & '89 (Prost), '88, '90 & '91 (Senna), '98 (Hakkinen)
Races contested: 476
Wins: 116

KEY PERSONNEL
Team principal: Ron Dennis
Technical director: Adrian Newey
Chief designer: Neil Oatley
Best 1998 results: 9 wins, 8 seconds, 3 thirds

Ron Dennis

1999 car:
McLaren-Mercedes MP4-14

Ferrari
Via Ascari 55-57
41053 Maranello
Modena
Italy
Tel: 39 536 949 111
Fax: 39 536 949 436

3 Michael Schumacher (D)

4 Eddie Irvine (GB)

1999 car:
Ferrari F399

The most evocative name in F1, Ferrari's prancing horse logo conjures images of exotic glamour. It is a combination of Modena yellow and the personal emblem of a World War 1 dogfight ace, Francesco Baracca, whose parents presented Enzo Ferrari with a shield identical to that carried by their son on his planes.

The company was formed by Enzo Ferrari in 1929 and originally prepared Alfa Romeos before building cars bearing its own name in the late forties. Froilan Gonzalez won Ferrari's first race in 1951 and then Alberto Ascari took back-to-back world championships in 1952-53.

The great Juan Manuel Fangio won the fourth of his five titles with Ferrari in 1956 and two years later Mike Hawthorn pipped Stirling Moss's Vanwall to the championship at the final race in Morocco.

The distinctive 156 'sharknose' saw Phil Hill become the first North American world champion in 1961 after team mate Taffy von Trips was killed at Monza. John Surtees became the first man to win world championships on two wheels and four with Ferrari in 1964 but it was then fully 11 years before Niki Lauda brought Ferrari its first championship success of the seventies. The Austrian followed up with another in 1977 and then South African Jody Scheckter repeated the feat in '79.

FERRARI

MILESTONES

Constructors' championship titles: 1961, '64, '75, '76, '77, '79, '82, '83
Drivers' championship titles: 1952 & '53 (Alberto Ascari), '56 (Fangio), '58 (Hawthorn), '61 (Phil Hill), '64 (Surtees), '75 & '77 (Lauda), '79 (Scheckter)
Races contested: 603
Wins: 119

KEY PERSONNEL

Sporting director: Jean Todt
Technical director: Ross Brawn
Chief designer: Rory Byrne
Best 1998 results: 6 wins, 5 seconds, 8 thirds

Ferrari has not won a drivers' championship since. The mega-buck signing of Michael Schumacher was designed to stop the rot, along with the recruitment of key ex-Benetton personnel from the German's championship years there. Although desperately close for the past two seasons, Michael is still chasing. Will this be the year?

Jean Todt

WILLIAMS

MILESTONES
Constructors' championship titles: 1980, '81, '86, '87, '92, '93, '94, '96, '97
Drivers' championship titles: 1980 (Jones), '82 (Rosberg), '87 (Piquet), '92 (Mansell), '93 (Prost), '96 (Hill), '97 (Villeneuve)
Races contested: 395
Wins: 103

Patrick Head

KEY PERSONNEL
Team principal: Frank Williams
Technical director: Patrick Head
Chief designers: Geoff Willis, Gavin Fisher
Best 1998 results: 3 thirds

Frank Williams was once the perennial underfinanced back-of-the-grid hard tryer. With live wire determination he progressed his business from one run out of the local telephone box to the ultra successful organisation that Williams Grand Prix Engineering is today.

Much of that is owed to the alliance with technical partner Patrick Head forged in 1976, 10 years before Frank himself was crippled in a car accident leaving a test session at Paul Ricard.

The Williams success really began with Saudi funding and Head's superb FW07 in the late seventies. Clay Regazzoni claimed the team's first win at Silverstone in 1979 and Alan Jones narrowly missed out on the championship, thanks in no small part to a revised scoring system.

Jones made amends the following season when the team also claimed its first constructors' championship, retained in 1981 although Carlos

Williams Grand Prix
Engineering
Grove
Wantage
Oxfordshire
OX12 0DQ
England
Tel: 44 (0) 1235 777700
Fax: 44 (0) 1235 764705

5 Alessandro Zanardi (I)

6 Ralf Schumacher (D)

1999 car:
Williams-Mecachrome FW21

Frank Williams

Reutemann lost the drivers' title to Nelson Piquet at the final race.

A Honda partnership yielded reward in the mid eighties, with Williams the dominant force of 1986-87, although Nigel Mansell's championship chances were dashed by the infamous Adelaide tyre blow-out just 18 laps from the end of the '86 season's final race.

Mansell finally got his reward in his second stint with the team six years later. His car, the active FW14B, was the most dominant seen in F1 since the ground effect Lotus 79 of 1978. By now Williams had Renault as its technical partner and continued to set the pace, with further titles falling to Alain Prost, Damon Hill and Jacques Villeneuve. Renault's withdrawal in 1997 was followed by the team's first winless season in a decade. The arrival of BMW for 2000 should see a rebirth but Zanardi and Schumacher face a tough battle this year.

Jordan Grand Prix
Buckingham Road
Silverstone
Northamptonshire
NN12 8TJ
England
Tel: 44 (0) 1327 857153
Fax: 44 (0) 1327 858120

7 Damon Hill (GB)

8 Heinz-Harald Frentzen (D)

1999 car:
Jordan-Mugen Honda 199

Prior to British American Racing, by far the most significant new arrival of the nineties was Jordan Grand Prix.

Eddie Jordan Racing, former winners of the British F3 title with Johnny Herbert in 1987 and then F3000 kings with Jean Alesi two years later, took the F1 plunge in time for the 1991 season. Gary Anderson's distinctive Jordan 191 was a lovely looking car and went just as well, Jordan benefiting from Ford's HB engine to finish fifth in the constructors' championship in a superb debut season.

But the Fords weren't free and Jordan was forced to sign a supply deal with Yamaha for 1992 if his team was to survive. The year was a disaster and 'the sewing machine' was one of the printable epithets applied to the Japanese V12. At the end of the season Jordan ran to Brian Hart for cover and in the second year with the Harlow manufacturer's underfinanced engine scored no fewer than 28 points with Rubens Barrichello and Eddie Irvine. The season included the team's first pole position, from Barrichello at a wet Spa.

A three-year deal with Peugeot for 1995 was supposed to project the team into the big time but the French elected to supply Alain Prost when he took over Ligier in 1997 and it was not until 1998 that Jordan scored its

JORDAN

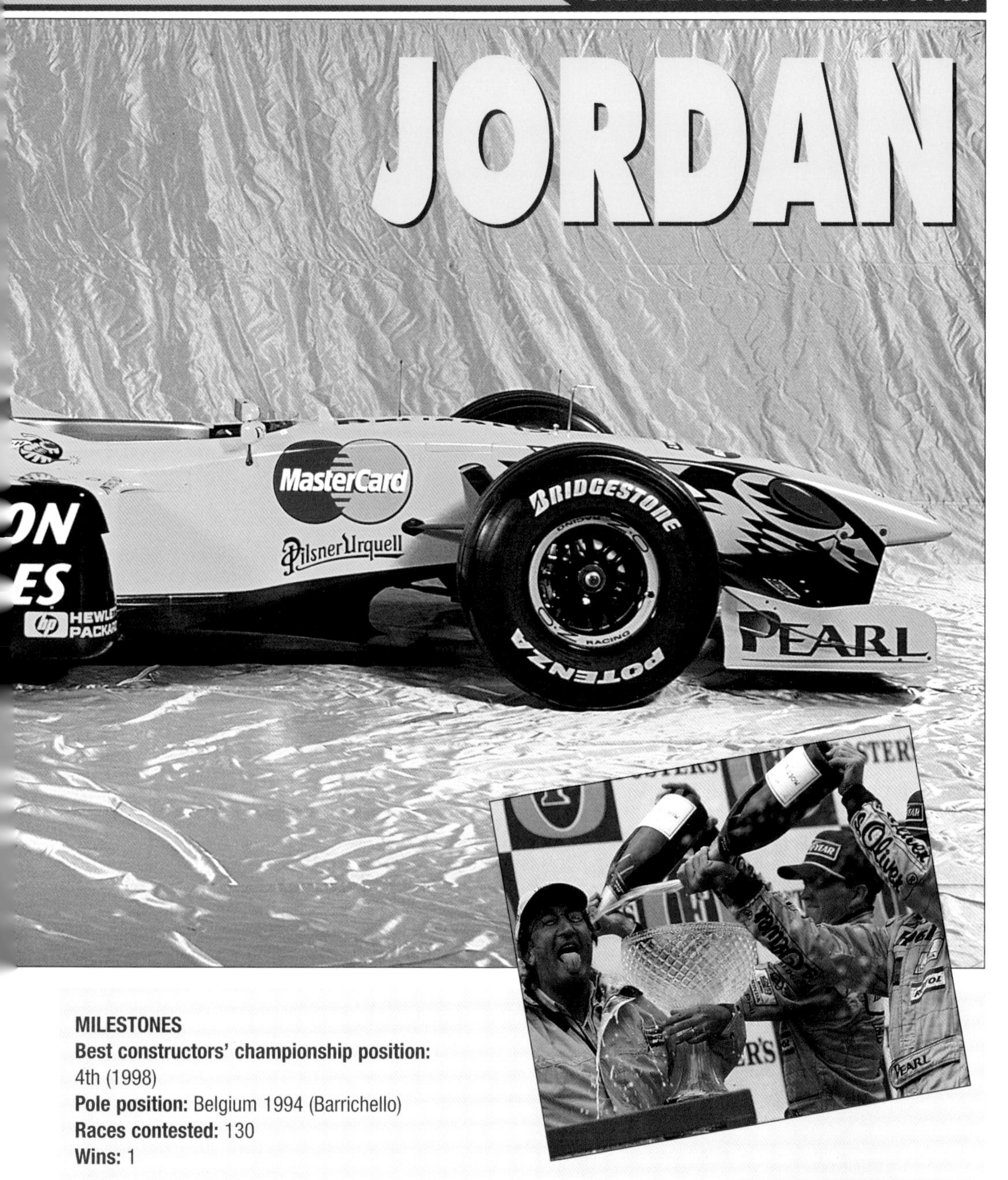

MILESTONES
Best constructors' championship position: 4th (1998)
Pole position: Belgium 1994 (Barrichello)
Races contested: 130
Wins: 1

KEY PERSONNEL
Team principal: Eddie Jordan **Managing director:** Trevor Foster
Technical director: Mike Gascoyne
Best 1998 results: 1 win, 1 second, 1 third

debut victory, with Mugen Honda power. Sponsorship from Benson & Hedges allowed the team to sign Damon Hill and, after an awful start to the season, Jordan pulled off one of the turnarounds of the decade, allowing Hill and Ralf Schumacher to score a 1-2 at a typically rain-afflicted Spa. The team was at last able to break the Williams—Ferrari—McLaren—Benetton 'Big Four' domination of F1.

Trevor Foster

BENETTON

MILESTONES
Constructors' championship title: 1995
Drivers' championship titles: 1994, '95 (Schumacher)
Races contested: 267
Wins: 26

KEY PERSONNEL
Team principal: Rocco Benetton
Technical director: Pat Symonds
Chief designer: Nick Wirth
Best 1998 results: 2 seconds

Rocco Benetton

Based in Treviso, northern Italy, Luciano Benetton saw F1 as the ideal medium for promoting his colourful apparel aimed at a young market. The company sponsored Tyrrell, Alfa Romeo and finally Toleman, which it bought in 1986.

The Benetton family had grand plans and the team started to emerge in the late eighties, becoming a serious force as the purpose-built Whiteways Technical Centre was established under Tom Walkinshaw's eye in time for 1992. Previously disparate parts of the company were brought together under one roof and it all coincided with Michael Schumacher's arrival in F1. The team poached Schumacher from Jordan and Benetton never looked back.

Although Williams stole a march technologically in the early nineties, Benetton responded well and in one season, 1993, mastered active ride, semi-automatic gearboxes

Benetton Formula
Whiteways Technical Centre
Enstone
Chipping Norton
Oxfordshire
OX7 4EE
England
Tel: 44 (0) 1608 678000
Fax: 44 (0) 1608 678609

9 Giancarlo Fisichella (I)

and traction control. Well-drilled operationally, they took control of the tragic 1994 season after Ayrton Senna was killed at Imola and Schumacher clinched the drivers' title in a controversial coming-together with Hill during the season finale in Adelaide. Williams, however, claimed the constructors' championship, something Benetton put right the following season, with Schumacher again the drivers' king.

Unsurprisingly, Schumacher's departure saw a steep dive in the Benetton performance level. The team endured a winless 1996 before Gerhard Berger finally stopped the rot at Hockenheim in 1997. Giancarlo Fisichella and Alexander Wurz represent F1's most promising young driver line-up, but with Renault withdrawing as official engine supplier in '97 and David Richards' tenure as main man lasting just a year, the team faces an uncertain future under Rocco Benetton.

Nick Wirth

10 Alexander Wurz (A)

1999 car:
Benetton-Supertec B199

PP Sauber AG
Wildbach Strasse 9
CH 8340 Hinwil
Switzerland
Tel: 41 1 9381400
Fax: 41 1 9381670

11 Jean Alesi (F)

12 Pedro Diniz (BR)

1999 car:
Sauber-Petronas C18

Peter Sauber started off tuning VW Beetles a stone's throw from the team's current Hinwil factory, while the first Sauber, the C1, was designed in the basement of his parents' apartment. The 'C' designation owes its root to the first initial of Sauber's wife, Christiane.

After some notable driving success Sauber concentrated on constructing, culminating in his running the programme for the official Mercedes return to sportscar racing from 1988. Highlights of the partnership included a double win at Le Mans and both the constructors' and drivers' world championships in 1989 and '90.

Sauber made an impressive switch to Formula 1 in 1993, scoring 12 points in its debut season with JJ Lehto and Karl Wendlinger. A serious accident at Monte Carlo in 1994 effectively ended Wendlinger's F1 career, however, and after two seasons of support from Mercedes, the three pointed star made an exclusive arrangement with McLaren.

Sauber then became the official works Ford team for two seasons and enjoyed some strong showings from Heinz-Harald Frentzen before losing the German to Williams. Energy drink producer Red Bull took a

MILESTONES
Best constructors' championship position: 6th (1993)
Races contested: 97
Best result: 3rd, Italy 1995 (Frentzen)

KEY PERSONNEL
Team principal: Peter Sauber **Technical director:** Leo Ress
Best 1998 result: 1 third

Peter Sauber

majority stakeholding in 1995, joined by Fritz Kaiser Group. Sauber's association with Jean Todt from sportscar days helped to secure a Ferrari engine deal, badged as a Petronas in a link-up with the team's new Malaysian partners.

Johnny Herbert in 1997 and Jean Alesi last year both turned in strong drives for Sauber but their first season still remains their best as the Swiss team continues to chase its first F1 victory.

MILESTONES
Best constructors' championship position: 4th (1988)
Pole position: USA (West) 1981 (Patrese)
Races contested: 321
Best result: 2nd, Sweden 1978, USA (West) 1980, San Marino 1981 (all Patrese), San Marino 1985 (Boutsen)

Tom Walkinshaw

KEY PERSONNEL
Team principals: Tom Walkinshaw, Prince Malik Ado Ibrahim **Technical director:** Mike Coughlan
Best 1998 results: 1 fourth, 1 fifth, 1 sixth

Heading into its 22nd season, Arrows boasts the unhappy record of having contested more races than any other winless team — 321.

Ironically, it came closest in its second ever race, when a young Riccardo Patrese convincingly led the 1978 South African Grand Prix until his engine expired.

Formed in 1977, the team went through the eighties without ever breaking into the ranks of the front-running British teams and, as the decade drew to a close, struck a deal with the Japanese Footwork corporation.

The Japanese funding did little to aid the team's competitiveness, however, and one of the original founders, Jackie Oliver (the others were Franco Ambrosio, Alan Rees and designers Dave Wass and Tony Southgate) regained control in 1995.

In March 1996, Oliver sold a major

ARROWS

Arrows Grand Prix
Leafield Technical Centre
Leafield
Nr Witney
Oxfordshire
OX8 5PF
England
Tel: 44 (0) 1993 871000
Fax: 44 (0) 1993 871400

14 Mika Salo (SF)

15 Pedro de la Rosa (E)

stakeholding to Tom Walkinshaw, who had by this time left Benetton. Walkinshaw had invested heavily in new premises, the former British Telecom training centre at Leafield, and pulled off a coup by signing reigning world champion Damon Hill for 1997 and recruiting design guru John Barnard as technical director.

The Arrows programme was hampered by both the logistics of combining the former Milton Keynes-based staff with Walkinshaw's TWR personnel and by an underpowered Yamaha engine. A disgruntled Hill left at the end of the year and Barnard was gone by mid '98.

Oliver has now sold his shares to owning triumvirate Walkinshaw, Prince Malik Ado Ibrahim and Morgan Grenfell Investment Bank.

At press time the '99 driver line-up was still undecided, although Spaniard Pedro de la Rosa was favourite to join Mika Salo.

Prince Malik Ado Ibrahim

1999 car:
Arrows A20

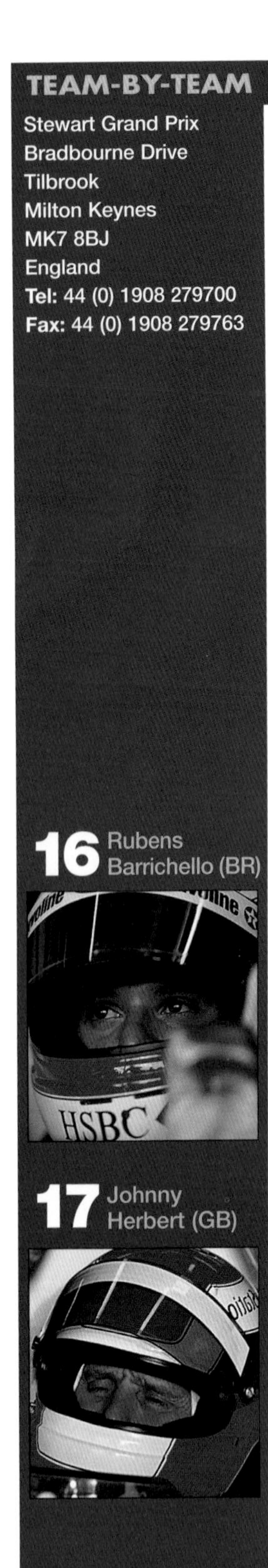

Stewart Grand Prix
Bradbourne Drive
Tilbrook
Milton Keynes
MK7 8BJ
England
Tel: 44 (0) 1908 279700
Fax: 44 (0) 1908 279763

16 Rubens Barrichello (BR)

17 Johnny Herbert (GB)

1999 car:
Stewart-Ford SF3

After winning 10 championships in the junior formulae, the Stewart family launched their Grand Prix project in 1996 and embarked on the trail as Ford's official works team at Melbourne in 1997.

Rubens Barrichello has been with the team from day one and scored an emotional second place at Monte Carlo in that first year. He was partnered by Jan Magnussen and much was expected of the young Dane after a record-breaking British F3 season with Paul Stewart Racing. Sadly for Magnussen, it didn't happen, and he was replaced mid 1998 by Dutchman Jos Verstappen. Verstappen now makes way for Johnny Herbert, the popular Briton joining after three years at Sauber.

The 1998 season brought eighth place in the constructors' championship, a disappointment for the team, and much speculation about Ford's continued involvement beyond the end of their four year commitment to the end of 2000. That was answered in the close season, however, when the Blue Oval announced a year's extension to the deal. High hopes are held for its new lightweight V10.

The team moved into new premises at Milton Keynes during the '98 season and strengthened its technical department over the winter with the recruitment of ex-Jordan designer Gary Anderson, who replaces the

STEWART

MILESTONES
Best constructors' championship position: 8th (1998)
Races contested: 33
Best result: 2nd, Monaco 1997 (Barrichello)

KEY PERSONNEL
Team principals: Jackie & Paul Stewart **Technical director:** Gary Anderson
Managing director: David Ring
Best 1998 results: 2 fifths, 1 sixth

departed Alan Jenkins as technical director.

Unlike Prost, which took over the Ligier operation, Stewart started from scratch and team principals Jackie and Paul both knew there would be no shortcuts. But, with the infrastructure now in place, 1999 is an important year for the team.

Jackie Stewart

PROST

MILESTONES
Best constructors' championship position: 6th (1997)
Races contested: 33
Best result: 2nd, Spain 1997 (Panis)

KEY PERSONNEL
Team principal: Alain Prost
Technical director: Loic Bigois
Best 1998 result: 1 sixth

Alain Prost

Four times world champion Alain Prost hung up his helmet after winning the last of his titles with Williams in 1993.

He took over the reins of the Ligier team at the end of 1996, with the equipe renamed Prost Grand Prix in time for the beginning of the 1997 season. 'Les Bleues' retained their traditional hue and were very much regarded as the French national team, although that is a label Prost is keen to quash in a global sponsorship market place.

Prost's first season coincided with the start of the Goodyear/Bridgestone tyre war and, with Mugen engines and Olivier Panis in the cockpit, Alain's team was the Japanese company's leading contender. Panis, an impressive winner at Monte Carlo in 1996 — admittedly amid fortunate circumstances — often looked a potential threat until suffering

Prost Grand Prix
Quartier des Sangliers
7 avenue Eugene
Freyssinet
78280 Guyancourt
France
Tel: 33 (0) 1 39301100
Fax: 33 (0) 1 39301101

18 Olivier Panis (F)

19 Jarno Trulli (I)

1999 car:
Prost-Peugeot AP02

John Barnard

fractures to both legs in a heavy accident in the Canadian Grand Prix at Montreal.

Prost's second season saw Peugeot involved as technical partner and the expectations rose. Sadly, though, 1998 was a disaster. The AP01 was not a good chassis and was further compromised by gearbox unreliability and the logistical problems caused by an early season factory move to the team's current facility at Guyancourt near Paris.

Prost and John Barnard go back to Alain's championship-winning days at McLaren and the design guru's recent announcement as technical consultant (through his 3D company in Guildford) is both logical and, Prost hopes, a problem solver.

Peugeot has now been in F1 five years without a win. That fact alone heaps extra pressure on the team.

Minardi Team SpA
Via Spallanzani No21
48018 Faenza
Italy
Tel: 39 546 696111
Fax: 39 546 620998

20 Marc Gene (E)

21 Shinji Nakano (J)

1999 car:
Minardi-Ford M01

Minardi are F1's minnows. Giancarlo Minardi, a true enthusiast, started constructing Formula 2 cars in time for the 1980 season and moved up to the top echelon five years later.

At the time, turbo engines were enjoying their F1 heyday and, after starting out wth a normally aspirated Cosworth, Minardi fielded the Motori Moderni turbo. The combination was way off the pace and poor Pierluigi Martini was the driver lumbered with it. Martini became almost part of the furniture at Minardi, driving on and off for 11 years. He scored the team's first point when he finished sixth at Detroit in 1988.

The following season represented a high point in Minardi's history as it made it into the championship top 10 for the first time, thereby qualifying for the lucrative FOCA travel benefits. Martini and Spaniard Luis Sala were both in the points at Silverstone and Martini finished fifth again at Estoril, where he actually led for a lap!

Deals to run Ferrari and Lamborghini engines in 1991 and '92 respectively did not produce the progress hoped for.

The 1998 season was the first of a three year plan which Minardi bosses Giancarlo Minardi and major shareholder Gabriele Rumi hope will turn the team into a serious outfit capable of challenging the big boys. The aim was to strengthen the team's human and technical assets

MILESTONES
Best constructors' championship position: 7th (1991)
Races contested: 221
Best result: 4th, San Marino & Portugal 1991, South Africa 1993 (all Martini)

KEY PERSONNEL
Team principals: Giancarlo Minardi, Gabriele Rumi
Technical director: Gustav Brunner
Best 1998 result: 1 seventh

Giancarlo Minardi

in 1998, to improve performance and results in '99 and then to launch a competitive car/engine/driver package in 2000 which will put the team among the leading contenders. It is a tall order.

At press time the '99 driver line-up was still fluid. Spaniard Marc Gene and last year's driver Shinji Nakano were still favourites, with Argentine Norberto Fontana and Ferrari tester and former F3000 champion Luca Badoer still possibles.

BAR

British American Racing was born out of an informal breakfast at Indianapolis in 1995. In the course of a casual conversation, Reynard founder, Adrian Reynard, fellow director, Rick Gorne, and Jacques Villeneuve's manager, Craig Pollock, found they shared a common dream: to move their successful association from Indy car competition into the Formula One arena.

Reynard, who already had experience of a Formula One project that had failed to come together properly, was adamant about his requirements for any such programme in which he and his company might become involved in the future. He would only make the move, he said, when he had total confidence in every aspect of the technical and financial package.

Together, the three men lobbied Tom Moser, who was behind the Player's Ltee backing of Jacques Villeneuve's highly successful Indy car campaign in North America. By the middle of 1997, the dream had become a reality and the group set about looking for an existing Grand Prix team to purchase in order to secure membership of Formula One's exclusive inner circle.

In late November 1997, they did just that, acquiring the famous Tyrrell Racing

KEY PERSONNEL

Managing director: Craig Pollock; **Technical director:** Adrian Reynard; **Commercial director:** Rick Gorne; **Chief designer:** Malcolm Oastler; **Chief engineer:** Steve Farrell; **Team manager:** Greg Field; **Test team manager:** Robert Synge

From left to right: Rick Gorne, Craig Pollock and Adrian Reynard

British American Racing
Operations Centre
Brackley
Northamptonshire
NN13 3BD
England
Tel: 44 (0) 1280 844001
Fax: 44 (0) 1280 840403

22 Jacques Villeneuve (CDN)

23 Ricardo Zonta (BR)

Organisation. The plan was that Tyrrell would operate normally during the 1998 season, and then be absorbed into the newly formed team the following year.

British American Racing, formed as the result of a partnership between Craig Pollock, Reynard Racing Cars and British American Tobacco, moved into stunning new headquarters near Brackley, Northamptonshire, in December last year and is now gearing up for its initial assault on Formula One. Also during 1998, the team signed reigning Formula One World Champion Villeneuve and FIA GT Champion Ricardo Zonta as drivers, and secured a supply of highly competitive Supertec V10 engines.

The first test will come at the Australian Grand Prix, in Melbourne, on March 7. There is no lack of racing know-how at British American Racing, and no one in the team is under any illusions about the size of the task that lies ahead. Whatever the challenges, though, excellence and achievement steadfastly remain the watchwords.

Malcolm Oastler

1999 car:
British American Racing-Supertec 01

British American Racing

The British American Racing-Supertec 01 launch confirmed that the exciting new team has concentrated on a simple, conventional design. The idea is to go racing with the minimum degree of complication.

The car ran for the first time at Barcelona on December 15, 1998. It was the realisation of a dream for British American Racing managing director Craig Pollock, although the 43-year-old suffered a scare when the team's private jet depressurised en route to the test!

The British American Racing dream became reality when the car tested for the first time at Barcelona on December 15, 1998.

The car's designer is Malcolm Oastler, an Australian with a lifelong interest in racing. Formerly runner-up in his national Formula Ford 1600 championship, Oastler earned a first-class honours degree from New South Wales University of Technology in Sydney. He joined Reynard Racing Cars in 1986 and has been responsible for championship-winning designs in

Presentation is all. British American Racing has a high tech new factory and equipment that will be up there with the best in any F1 paddock.

Formula Ford 2000, Formula 3, Formula 3000 and Indy car/Champ Car racing.

Oastler describes his latest creation as 'state-of-the-art, but as simple as we could make it. A lot has to happen with a new race team,' he says. 'All the systems, right down to how we get to a meeting and unload the truck, need to be established. If we had a complicated car with complicated systems, it would be that much more difficult. We need to go racing, pure and simple. We'll add complication as necessary.'

British American Racing has an advantage over recent new teams in that technical director Adrian Reynard has almost 20 years of production know-how on which to call.

'There is a very good infrastructure,' Oastler says. 'You know who to give a drawing to, what's going to happen next and how it all flows through the place. That's as much of a challenge as the design side. The drawing office generates the first car. After that, making sure that you generate the second, the third, and replace all the bits that become lifed out, is what takes the work.'

Oastler denies, however, that the task presented by a Grand Prix car is anything out of the ordinary: 'In some ways, a Champ Car is actually more of a challenge because you have to cover such a broad spectrum of events.'

Tyre supply problems meant that British American Racing and Oastler were denied the luxury of a private shakedown test for their new creation. Instead, the British American Racing-Supertec 01 had a public baptism in front of an expectant media in Spain. Promisingly, Villeneuve lapped in the low 1m 23s bracket at Barcelona after experiencing the expected teething troubles, including the engine cover flying off.

'When pieces came off, I began to panic...'

'When pieces came off — starting with the rear wing and then the engine cover — I began to panic,' Pollock admits. 'The only person who didn't was Jacques. He stopped the car in one piece and walked into the garage with a glint in his eye, looked me straight in the face, and said:

Jacques Villeneuve was excited by the new car's potential from the first time he took the wheel.

"Well, she's fast." '

'At least we managed to fix the problems and carry on,' Oastler adds. 'When the car was running it showed promise. We did a lap-and-a-half, then had a gearbox bearing problem. Then there was a wheel bearing assembly issue. You miss a day-and-a-half dealing with things like that, but when Jacques did a low 1m 23s lap, I was impressed.'

So was team manager Greg Field: 'All the top teams were there, except Ferrari. We did about 30 laps, of which eight were timed, and we ended up third fastest overall. I think that's an incredible achievement.'

Flavio Briatore — back on the Grand Prix scene as boss of engine supplier Supertec.

Much has been made of Adrian Reynard's claims that he doesn't like to enter a new formula without hopes of winning the first race, something his company has managed in every category it has entered. Pollock, however, is more realistic about the team's aims for F1.

'Our goal is to become the most professional team in the pit lane. If we can achieve that, there is no reason why the results can't follow. It has been a humbling and uplifting experience to be involved with so many dedicated individuals, all experts in their own field.' The British American Racing operation already numbers more than 200. Although slightly short of McLaren/Ferrari/ Williams levels, it is nevertheless 50 in excess of Jordan Grand Prix.

Going into the new season, there is an unmistakably bullish air about the new team. Villeneuve, justifying his decision to leave Williams in order to join British American Racing, explains: 'There is a gust of fresh air. If you've got the right technology, the right budgets and the right frame of mind, there's every chance you can win. Most teams go into F1 wanting to finish at least 10th, so they are not going to do better than that. Also, I'd been at Williams three years and didn't want to do another interim year.

'If I didn't believe we could be competitive at

Better by design

Adrian Reynard is confident that British American Racing's new, state-of-the-art Brackley factory will give it an operational advantage over rival F1 teams.

Says Reynard: 'I designed the current Benetton factory, having previously planned it for the Formula 1 project which Reynard abandoned in the early 1990s. The new British American Racing factory is far more efficient. It is made in wings, primarily for flexibility and access.

'The race team area is laid out so that things can come straight out of the truck and into bays, flowing through to be broken down into sub-assembly groups for rebuild.

'The race team modules work exactly as they do in the pits, right down to the plug-in sockets for air, data acquisition, etc. Data, instead of going back to the truck as it does at the track, goes straight to the right people's drawing office or to the wind tunnel.

'The drawing office might look like a conventional drawing office, but it's really a whole technical area. Design, development, aerodynamics, even purchasing, are all together. That's important. You don't want someone to design something they can't buy. Everyone works in the same area so that communication is easy and everything can be done quickly. The factory has been designed as the most efficient manufacturing machine I can think of.'

Adrian Reynard has 20 years' experience of racing car production techniques.

Reynard has been strongly involved in personnel recruitment and says: 'We concentrated on people with the right attitude and a killer instinct. One of the qualities is ambition. It's a highly ambitious game, but I've never known that setting one's targets too high is a bad thing.

'We received 2000 applications. We were looking for people prepared to take large amounts of responsibility and make decisions without massive amounts of supervision. That type of structure is the way we will move forward faster than the opposition, not just on the technical side, but also on the management side.

'What I hope we've done at British American Racing is take all the best Reynard practices. This factory has been designed based on my 20 years' experience of making production racing cars. Believe me, I think it's the epitome — the most efficient design to manufacture plant that you could ever want in Formula 1.'

Reynard considers BAR's new factory to be 'the most efficient design to manufacture plant that you could ever want'.

Zonta watches as Villeneuve tries out the new car — and looks forward to his F1 debut.

British American Racing, I wouldn't have joined. The people are also a factor. When you are going to spend most of your life working with the same people, it's important to have a good relationship at every level. Also, once you are part of a team for a while, it's always an evolution. It becomes difficult to have new ideas.'

The Renault V10 was widely regarded as the best engine in Grand Prix racing between 1991 and 1997. Responsibility for marketing of the Renault Sport-developed Formula 1 engines has now passed to Supertec Sport, and company

Craig Pollock

Craig Pollock was born in Scotland in 1956. He originally taught physical education in Keith before spending two years in business. Returning to physical education, he taught at a top Swiss private school, where one of his pupils was the 12-year-old Jacques Villeneuve.

Pollock left education in the mid 1980s and became involved in a number of Japanese and European business interests before Villeneuve sought him out to manage his racing affairs in 1993.

The relationship with Adrian Reynard and Rick Gorne began in Indy cars, with the Formula 1 plan crystallising as Villeneuve won both the Indy car title and the blue riband Indy 500 in Reynard machinery. When British American Racing came together in November 1997, Pollock was on board as managing director.

Zonta explores the car's impressive grip and balance during an early test session.

boss Flavio Briatore confirmed at the British American Racing launch that there will be an ongoing development schedule throughout 1999. Adrian Reynard expressed confidence that Renault Sport technicians were hungry to see the new Supertec FB01 engine back at the top.

For his part, the highly experienced Briatore is full of praise for the new team. 'For me, British American Racing has all of the ingredients to be one of the top names in Formula 1 in the near future,' he says. 'It's dynamic, innovative and aggressive in its approach, as well as being very

Adrian Reynard

Adrian Reynard, 48, built his first racing car in 1973 as a student project and joined British Leyland as a project engineer a year later.

Reynard Racing Cars was founded in 1977 and, no mean driver himself, Reynard won a European Formula Ford 2000 title the following year. In 1979, his cars won both the British and European FF2000 Championships.

The Reynard design team has the unique distinction of having won the first race in every major single-seater championship in which it has competed — including Formula 3, Formula 3000 and Indy cars.

Reynard cars have won the Indy 500 twice and have dominated the USA's major single-seater series for the past four years. The company also carries out consultancy work for Ford, Chrysler, Honda and Toyota, and has twice been honoured with the Queen's Award for export achievement.

The BAR project has evolved from idea status into the sport's most exciting new team, with over 200 employees, in little more than a year.

strong technically and commercially. Craig Pollock and his team are as motivated, focused and committed to winning as we are at Supertec, so we feel very comfortable working with them.'

British American Racing's arrival in Formula 1 has not all been plain sailing, however, the sport's governing body, the FIA, taking exception to the team's plan to run its two cars in completely different liveries in 1999 (Lucky Strike for Villeneuve and State Express 555 for FIA GT Champion Ricardo Zonta). The FIA claimed this approach contravened a regulation passed last September, requiring all Formula 1 teams to present their cars in substantially the same livery. Pollock disagreed and took the matter to the International Court of Arbitration. The arbitrators subsequently found in favour of the FIA position and, at the time of writing, British American Racing personnel were redesigning the livery of the team's cars to comply with the regulation. Villeneuve, though, will continue to be designated as the Lucky Strike driver and Zonta as 555's man.

The Lucky Strike brand is regarded as particularly apt for Villeneuve. It has been around for 125 years and the current pack, designed by Raymond Loewy in 1942, is widely viewed as a design classic. The brand is often associated with non-conformists, free thinkers and individuals who refuse to follow the herd. If that description applies to anyone in the F1 paddock, it is undoubtedly Villeneuve.

By comparison, State Express 555's chosen driver, Ricardo Zonta, fits perfectly with that brand's history of taking on new challenges and helping nurture up-and-coming talent, the most recent example being Colin McRae's success with

Malcolm Oastler

Chief designer Malcolm Oastler finished runner-up in the Australian Formula Ford 1600 championship in his rookie year before coming to Britain in the hope of pursuing a driving career.

In possession of a first-class honours degree from NSW University of Technology in Sydney, however, he soon realised his talents were better suited to the drawing board and joined Reynard full time in 1986.

Since then, he has collaborated with Adrian Reynard on the company's first Formula 3000 chassis, his designs going on to win five championships in as many years. He then continued his success and led Reynard's Indy car design team, with the 95I chassis winning eight races, including the Indy 500, and starting from pole position 13 times. Logically, Formula 1 was the next challenge.

the 555 Subaru team in the FIA World Rally Championship.

Despite the difficulty with dual liveries, however, Adrian Reynard has converted the issue into a positive as far as team efficiency is concerned: 'It has actually been a stimulus,' he observes. 'At the beginning, we had to say, okay, how can we improve our painting process? Teams paint their cars in a certain way, and because our original plan was to have cars in two different liveries, we had to come up with a method of painting ours in half the time. Now, even though we won't be able to run the cars in that form, we have learned how to paint them quicker and without any loss in quality. That's got to be a good thing.'

Rick Gorne

Rick Gorne, British American Racing's commercial director, was also a promising driver before a leg-breaking accident brought his career to a premature end. Gorne hit a tree at Ingliston in a car sponsored by Barratt Builders, whose logo was...an oak tree.

Gorne joined Reynard as sales manager in 1982, and was made a director within a week. Rising to managing director, he has been largely responsible for the commercial success of Reynard on both sides of the Atlantic.

During 1998, Gorne concentrated on three main areas: devising a long-term strategy for potential sponsors; ensuring that British American Racing was a success from a business standpoint, and overseeing all human resource aspects of the new team. He regards a young, motivated work force and solid communications as vital ingredients of Reynard's success.

THE DRIVERS

BELL
DVAG
Marlboro
Marlboro

Mika HAKKINEN (SF)

Age: 30 (28/9/68)
Born: Helsinki (SF)
GPs: 112
Wins: 9
Poles: 10
Fastest laps: 7
Points: 218

Hakkinen's 1998 world championship success was no more than those who witnessed his early career expected. The Finn won the inaugural GM Lotus Euroseries title in his first year of racing in the UK, then went on to claim the British F3 title in 1990.

He shot straight into F1 with Lotus and finished eighth in the world championship for Hethel in 1992. McLaren and Williams both fought over his signature for '93 in front of the contracts recognition board. By the time McLaren boss Ron Dennis won the day he already had Ayrton Senna and Michael Andretti under contract. Hakkinen sat out the year testing until Andretti left post-Monza, whereupon Mika outqualified Senna in his first race for the team! His eight wins in 1998 were a result of getting his hands on his first competitive F1 car.

Age: 27 (27/3/71)
Born: Twynholm (GB)
GPs: 74
Wins: 4
Poles: 8
Fastest laps: 8
Points: 173

David COULTHARD (GB)

Coulthard is another driver to have a meteoric rise through the junior formulae, bringing him a Williams test contract for 1994. He graduated to the race team in tragic circumstances following Ayrton Senna's death at Imola. After 18 months alongside Damon Hill, bringing his first win in Portugal and four consecutive poles, Coulthard lost his drive to Jacques Villeneuve but went straight into another top seat at McLaren.

After McLaren's three year hiatus, Coulthard broke the team's barren spell at Melbourne in 1997, the first race in West colours, and won again at Monza. Hakkinen is a tough proposition as a team mate, however, and one win against Mika's eight in 1998 makes '99 a crucial year for the Scot.

Michael SCHUMACHER (D)

Age: 30 (3/1/69)
Born: Kerpen (D)
GPs: 118
Wins: 33
Poles: 20
Fastest laps: 35
Points: 526

The yardstick by which all others are judged.

Served notice that he was something very special when he qualified seventh on his debut for Jordan at Spa in 1991. Poached by Benetton he immediately outpaced triple champion Nelson Piquet and took the first of two successive titles in 1994 after Senna's fatal accident. Assumed the Brazilian's crown as king of F1 and joined Ferrari in 1996 with a salary to match.

Drove superbly in inferior machinery in 1997 but lost out to Jacques Villeneuve in controversial circumstances at the last round. Tarnished his reputation badly but rebuilt it with another superb year in 1998 which ultimately saw him pipped at the post again by Mika Hakkinen, though in much more sporting fashion.

Age: 33 (10/11/65)
Born: Newtownards (GB)
GPs: 81
Wins: 0
Poles: 0
Fastest laps: 0
Points: 99

Eddie IRVINE (GB)

His own tenacity earned plum drives in the junior categories, which Irvine used well to fully demonstrate his potential. When funds ran dry in Europe in 1990 he made the move to the then lucrative Japanese F3000 scene before Eddie Jordan brought him into the F1 arena at Suzuka in 1993. A dust-up with Ayrton Senna and then a racing incident for which he shouldered the blame in the first race of 1994 earned him an unfair reputation as a wild man.

Spent much of his junior career around James Hunt which further developed a natural irreverence and did nothing to foster any fondness for political correctness. Better than he's given credit for, as 1998 consistency showed, but cast in thankless role of supporting Schumacher. Hopes to break win drought somewhere along the line in 1999.

Alessandro ZANARDI (I)

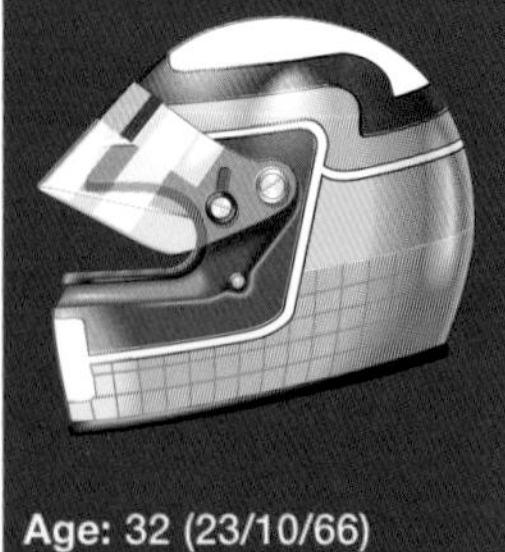

Age: 32 (23/10/66)
Born: Rome (I)
GPs: 25
Wins: 0
Poles: 0
Fastest laps: 0
Points: 1

A former Italian F3 Champion, Zanardi finished runner-up in the 1991 FIA F3000 Championship and made his F1 debut the same season in place of the imprisoned Bertrand Gachot at Jordan.

Forced to sit out most of 1992 through lack of funding, he returned with Lotus in '93 and was fortunate to survive an enormous accident at Spa. He lost his seat to Pedro Lamy but returned to the underfinanced Lotus operation when Lamy was injured in testing.

A move to the USA finally gave Zanardi the chance to show his true class and back-to-back Champ Car titles were the result. Pedigree deserves a Williams drive, but is it the right time to be there?

Age: 23 (30/6/75)
Born: Huerth (D)
GPs: 33
Wins: 0
Poles: 0
Fastest laps: 0
Points: 27

Ralf SCHUMACHER (D)

Doubters suspected that his F1 ticket came as a result of the right surname and initially there was not a great deal to prove them wrong. Headstrong and hard to control in his early days at Jordan, he was involved in a battle for superiority with Fisichella.

Quick but prone to accidents, his most high profile incident came at Nurburgring where he took his brother out at the first corner in a move which could arguably have cost Michael the title that year.

Unfazed by Hill in year two, Schumacher Jr started to emerge in the second half of 1998 and played his part in Jordan's 1-2 finish at Spa. Impressed the team with his pace and attitude in pre-season tests.

Damon HILL (GB)

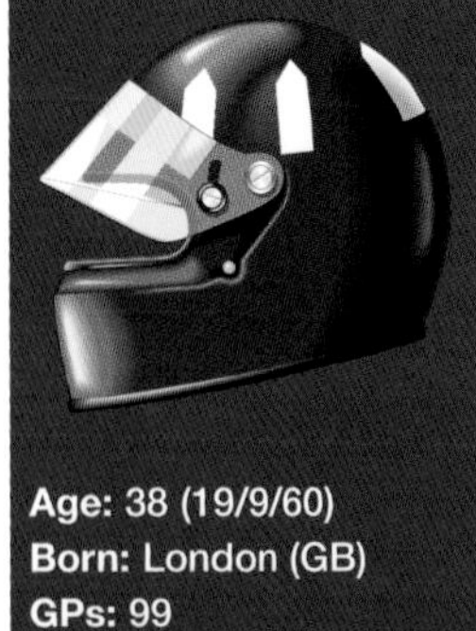

Age: 38 (19/9/60)
Born: London (GB)
GPs: 99
Wins: 22
Poles: 20
Fastest laps: 19
Points: 353

Like his double world champion father, Damon was a latecomer to motor racing. His career in the junior formulae was good rather than exceptional but his attitude and testing abilities were much admired by Williams and earned him a full time seat alongside Alain Prost in 1993.

It was a superb debut season, Damon scoring a hat-trick of wins before Prost retired and Ayrton Senna arrived. When Senna was killed early in '94, the burden of leading the team fell on Hill's shoulders. He rose to the task superbly, faltered in '95 and then bounced back to win the championship in 1996. His reward was the loss of his contract and tough seasons at Arrows and Jordan followed. Brought Jordan its first victory at rainy Spa last year and has high hopes for '99.

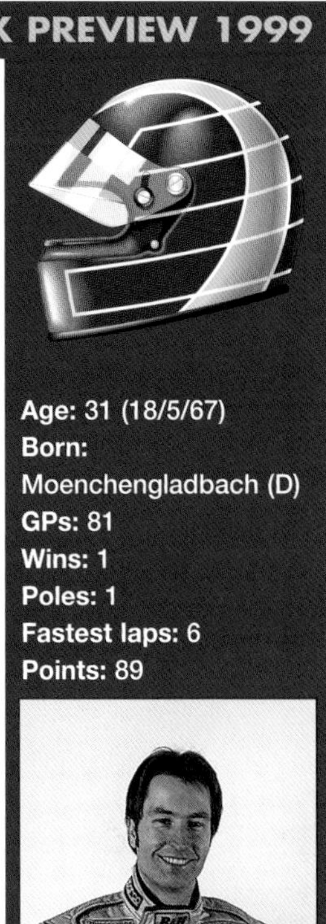

Age: 31 (18/5/67)
Born: Moenchengladbach (D)
GPs: 81
Wins: 1
Poles: 1
Fastest laps: 6
Points: 89

Heinz-Harald FRENTZEN (D)

Touted as a match for Michael Schumacher during his days alongside the future double champion in the Sauber-Mercedes sportscar line-up, Frentzen made his F1 debut with Sauber in 1994. He was immediately quick and brought the car home in the points four times, including a fourth place at Magny Cours.

Frank Williams approached Frentzen in the aftermath of Senna's death and was impressed by the German's loyalty in staying at Sauber. He was rewarded with a Williams seat for 1997, controversially ousting reigning champion Hill, but his two seasons at Grove were disappointing, netting just a lone win at Imola. Expect an entertaining battle with Hill for Jordan supremacy in '99.

Giancarlo FISICHELLA (I)

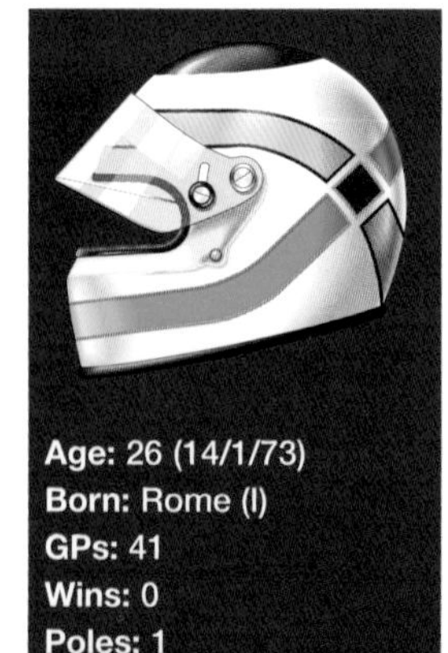

Age: 26 (14/1/73)
Born: Rome (I)
GPs: 41
Wins: 0
Poles: 1
Fastest laps: 1
Points: 36

A former Italian F3 Champion, Fisichella was hailed as Italy's new coming man when he made his F1 debut with Minardi in 1996 before forming half of an inexperienced Jordan line-up in 1997.

With Ralf Schumacher equally keen to make his mark, the early races brought fireworks and the young team mates actually collided in Argentina. Eddie Jordan read the riot act and the performances matured, with Fisichella very close to a win at Hockenheim.

Giancarlo switched to Benetton for 1998 and scored fine second places at Monte Carlo and Montreal and took pole in Austria. A definite front runner given a competitive technical package.

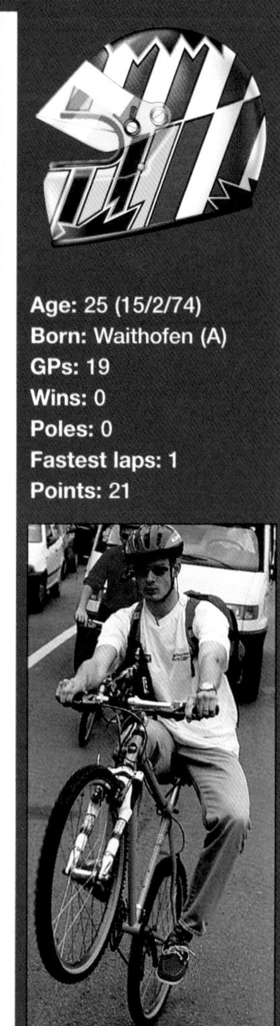

Age: 25 (15/2/74)
Born: Waithofen (A)
GPs: 19
Wins: 0
Poles: 0
Fastest laps: 1
Points: 21

Alexander WURZ (A)

Son of multiple rallycross champion Franz Wurz, Alexander earned his chance in F1 via some strong sportscar performances, including victory in the Le Mans 24 Hours, and impressive testing performances for Benetton.

Hailed by Austrians as the new Niki Lauda, Wurz shares Lauda's interest in the technical side of racing and is both focused and intelligent. His Benetton race debut in place of the unfit Gerhard Berger in 1997 brought podium performances and a wake up call for Jean Alesi. Promotion to the race team followed, where Wurz and new signing Giancarlo Fisichella proved incredibly closely matched. Wheelbanging with Schumacher at Monaco proved he is not afraid of reputations.

Jean ALESI (F)

Age: 34 (11/6/64)
Born: Avignon (F)
GPs: 151
Wins: 1
Poles: 2
Fastest laps: 4
Points: 233

Alesi burst onto the F1 scene in 1989, the same year that he took the F3000 International Championship for Eddie Jordan Racing.

Suddenly without a driver, Ken Tyrrell put Alesi in at Paul Ricard and was astounded when Jean ran second and finished fourth! That earned him a seat for the rest of the year and, pre-Schumacher, Alesi became F1's new hot property. At one stage in 1990 he had three signed contracts in his briefcase, with Tyrrell, Ferrari and Williams.

Unsurprisingly given his Sicilian blood, Ferrari won the day and Alesi spent the next five seasons at Maranello. How different things may have been if he'd signed for Frank... Two disappointing seasons at Benetton followed before Alesi joined Sauber for 1998.

Age: 28 (22/5/70)
Born: Sao Paulo (BR)
GPs: 66
Wins: 0
Poles: 0
Fastest laps: 0
Points: 7

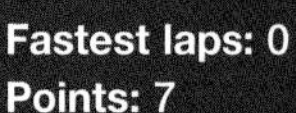

Pedro DINIZ (BR)

Diniz made his Grand Prix debut in his home race at Interlagos in 1995. He joined the uncompetitive Forti team and suffered as a result, in much the same way that Pierluigi Martini did with Minardi a decade earlier. Diniz's problem was compounded by being moneyed, which caused no-one to take him seriously as a driver.

In fact, he is way better than widely appreciated. In 1997 he outqualified reigning world champion Arrows team mate Damon Hill at demanding drivers' circuits like Spa and Suzuka and was only a gnat's whisker away at Monte Carlo. He did much the same to the highly touted Mika Salo last year and impressed in initial testing with Sauber.

Mika SALO (SF)

Age: 32 (30/11/66)
Born: Helsinki (SF)
GPs: 67
Wins: 0
Poles: 0
Fastest laps: 0
Points: 15

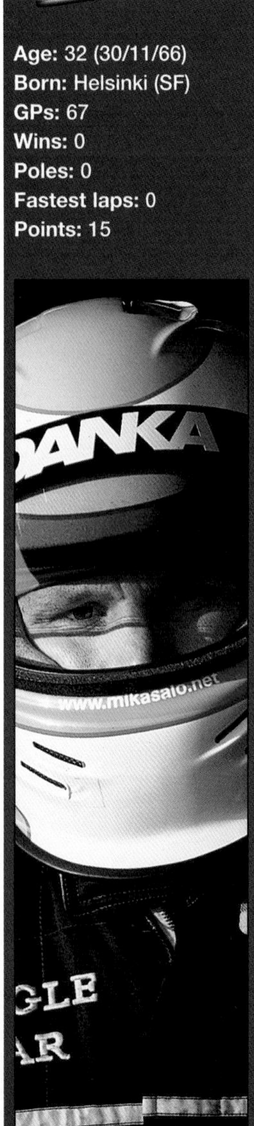

Salo, like Hakkinen pre-'98, is another highly rated Finn awaiting an opportunity in a competitive car.

The two Finns fought hard for the British F3 title in 1990 before economic considerations forced Salo to pursue his career in Japan. He got his Grand Prix chance with Lotus at the end of 1994, doing the final two races, but the team was just about to call in the administrators.

From there it was three seasons at Tyrrell, generally in decent chassis suffering from engines that were unreliable, underpowered or both. Arrows has not turned out to be the progression he hoped and Salo is in need of a break.

Age: 28 (24/2/71)
Born: Barcelona (E)
GPs: 0
Wins: 0
Poles: 0
Fastest laps: 0
Points: 0

Pedro DE LA ROSA (E)

De la Rosa was 16 before he convinced his father to buy him a kart, by which time he already had two European titles under his belt — for radio-control competitions! He won the Spanish Formula Fiat championship in his first season of full competition, then raced in British F3 before a move east netted him the All-Japan F3 title in 1995, with eight wins. He also finished third at Macau that year, behind Ralf Schumacher and Jarno Trulli. In 1997 he won the All-Japan Formula Nippon and GT championships in the same year and was contracted by Jordan as test and reserve driver for 1998. Backed by Repsol, he was favourite for the second Arrows seat as this guide closed for press.

Rubens BARRICHELLO (BR)

Age: 26 (23/5/72)
Born: Sao Paulo (BR)
GPs: 96
Wins: 0
Poles: 1
Fastest laps: 0
Points: 56

Barrichello enjoyed a brilliant career in the junior formulae, winning the EFDA GM Lotus Euroseries before claiming the British F3 Championship at his first attempt. He finished third in the FIA F3000 series and went on to make his Grand Prix debut with Jordan as a 20-year-old in 1993. He was heading for a potential podium in the rain-afflicted European GP at Donington — his third race — before the car failed.

Always a star performer in the wet, Barrichello took full advantage of similar conditions at Monte Carlo to bring tears to new team boss Jackie Stewart's eyes with second place behind Michael Schumacher in the team's debut season after four years at Jordan. Reunited with old ex-Jordan pal/engineer Gary Anderson.

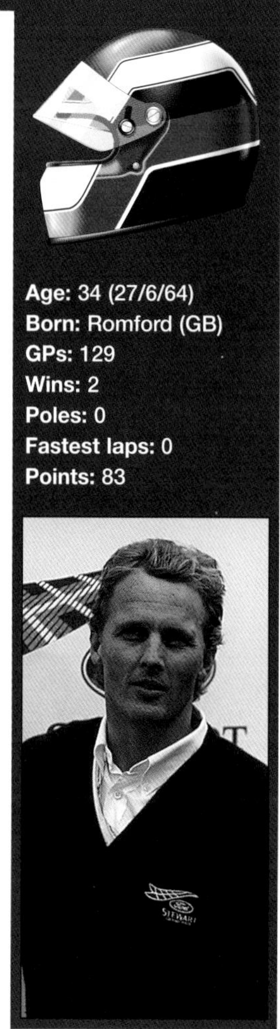

Age: 34 (27/6/64)
Born: Romford (GB)
GPs: 129
Wins: 2
Poles: 0
Fastest laps: 0
Points: 83

Johnny HERBERT (GB)

Johnny Herbert was the blond young rising British superstar of the mid eighties. A Formula Ford Festival winner and British F3 Champion with Eddie Jordan, he astounded experienced F1 observers with his tests for Benetton and Lotus and was hailed as the greatest British talent since Jim Clark. Sadly, an enormous F3000 accident at Brands Hatch in 1988 almost ended Herbert's career before it had truly begun.

Johnny still walks with a limp and freely admits that lack of mobility in the ankle means that he is not the driver he was. The advent of semi-automatic gearboxes effectively saved his career and he was still good enough to win the British and Italian GPs with Benetton in 1995. Of the current drivers, only former Sauber team mate Jean Alesi has more experience. A tough year alongside Barrichello at Stewart?

Olivier PANIS (F)

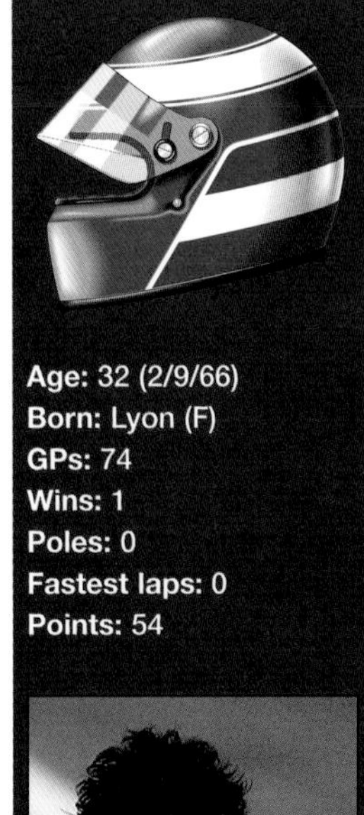

Age: 32 (2/9/66)
Born: Lyon (F)
GPs: 74
Wins: 1
Poles: 0
Fastest laps: 0
Points: 54

Alesi has Sicilian blood, which leaves Olivier as the only true Frenchman in F1, a follower of the well trodden Elf path.

Panis won the FIA F3000 Championship in 1993, earning himself a seat at Ligier. He scored a fortuitous second place at Hockenheim and achieved further points finishes in Hungary and Australia.

Always consistent, Panis finished eighth in the 1995 championship, ending the season with another second place in the final Adelaide Grand Prix, albeit two laps down on Damon Hill. His career highlight came the following year with a fighting win in Monte Carlo but 1997 brought a leg-breaking accident in Canada. Frustrated by the unreliable Prost AP01 last season and in need of a good year.

Age: 24 (13/7/74)
Born: Pescara (I)
GPs: 30
Wins: 0
Poles: 0
Fastest laps: 0
Points: 4

Jarno TRULLI (I)

With Fisichella, regarded as the future of top level Italian motor racing.

Trulli was a karting superstar whose rise through the ranks has been meteoric. From karts he went straight into F3, winning the German championship, and after being picked up by Flavio Briatore was installed at Minardi before being switched to Prost when Olivier Panis broke his legs in Canada.

Sensationally led the 1997 Austrian Grand Prix in unflustered manner before being overhauled by Villeneuve. Focused and intelligent, he looks set for a top class future but suffered a frustrating 1998 with difficult, unreliable machinery.

Marc GENE (E)

Age: 24 (29/3/74)
Born: Sabadell (E)
GPs: 0
Wins: 0
Poles: 0
Fastest laps: 0
Points: 0

The younger brother of former Benetton tester Jordi, Marc Gene comes to Minardi with healthy funding from Telefonica, the Spanish telecommunications network. He started karting at the age of eight and collected a plethora of national titles. Went on to finish runner-up in the Formula Ford Festival before spending two seasons in British F3. Made the move to Formula 3000 in 1997 and then scooped the Open Fortuna championship with six wins and three pole positions en route. Impressed Giancarlo Minardi in test drive last year. The only driver on the grid with a degree, in economics, from Buckingham University, presented to him by Margaret Thatcher!

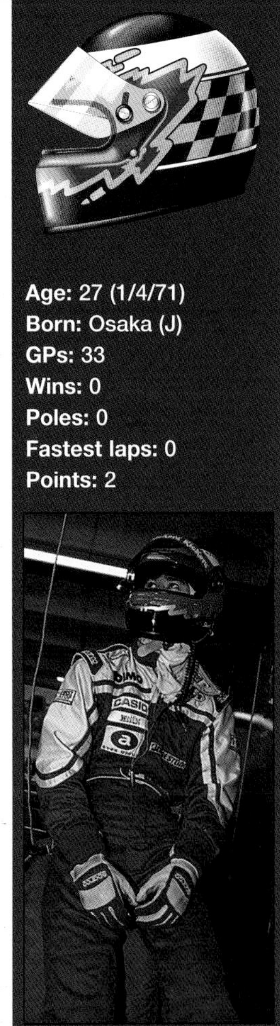

Age: 27 (1/4/71)
Born: Osaka (J)
GPs: 33
Wins: 0
Poles: 0
Fastest laps: 0
Points: 2

Shinji NAKANO (J)

After the departure of Aguri Suzuki and Ukyo Katayama and prior to the arrival of Toranosuke Takagi, Nakano was Japan's sole representative in F1. There was no stunning record in the junior categories but his first season of F1, in 1997 with Prost, was competent. He finished sixth at Hungaroring and was unfazed by the highly touted Trulli, whom he outpaced occasionally. A move to Minardi for '98 placed him with Esteban Tuero but neither man was able to shine with the machinery available. At press time he was negotiating to retain his seat but faced competition from Luca Badoer and Norberto Fontana.

Jacques VILLENEUVE (CDN)

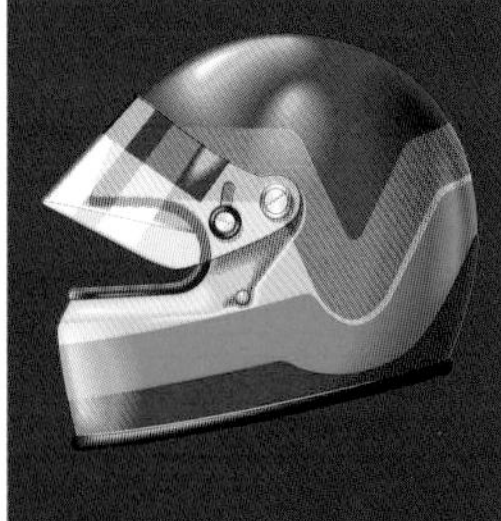

Age: 27 (9/4/71)
Born; St Jean sur Richelieu
GPs: 49
Wins: 11
Poles: 13
Fastest laps: 9
Points: 180

Enjoyed the enviable position of making his F1 debut with Williams in the best car of 1996. CART title and victory in the Indy 500 of '95 set him up for the plum drive. Could not quite match Damon Hill in that first year, but nevertheless took the championship down to the wire.

With Hill departed, Villeneuve led the Williams assault in 1997 and, showing the same spirit and competitive instinct as his late father, won the championship in fine style in a head-to-head finale with Schumacher at Jerez. His decisive overtaking move was brilliantly opportunistic.

The 1998 season was a rude awakening as Williams slipped from the top of the pile and the reigning champ endured a winless year. Sees British American Racing challenge as a gust of fresh air.

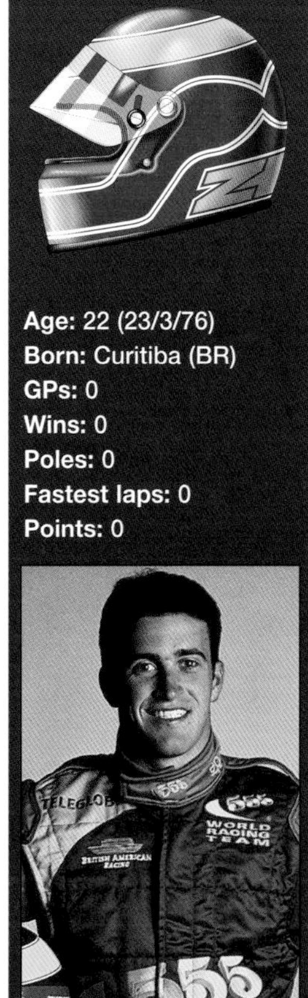

Age: 22 (23/3/76)
Born: Curitiba (BR)
GPs: 0
Wins: 0
Poles: 0
Fastest laps: 0
Points: 0

Ricardo ZONTA (BR)

The new British American Racing team is seen as an ideal environment for Ricardo Zonta to make his F1 debut. The team might be new but it has many experienced top line racing personnel, is copiously funded and, with a Supertec V10, should boast enviable reliability. Zonta can look forward to racing miles and come the second half of the season may well be challenging team leader Jacques Villeneuve.

The Brazilian won the FIA F3000 Championship in 1997 and is the reigning GT champion after a superb season with Mercedes-Benz. He also impressed McLaren with his test work for the team and is set to emerge as a future star.

THE CIRCUITS

Albert Park, Melbourne

(3.294 miles) 58 laps

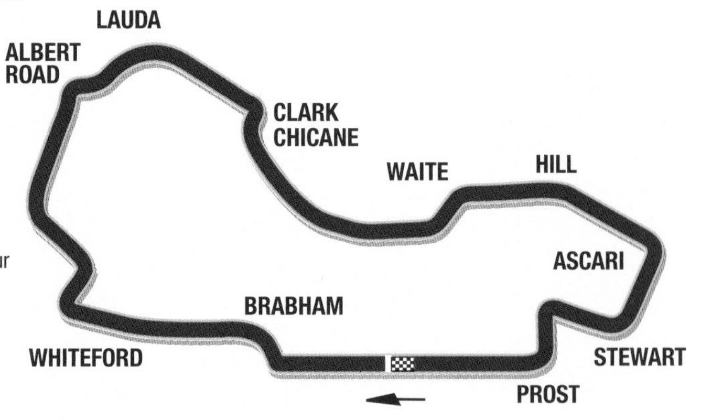

LAST YEAR

McLaren showed crushing superiority as Mika Hakkinen and David Coulthard lapped the entire field en route to a debut 1-2 success for the new MP4-13. Controversy reigned, however, as race leader Hakkinen misinterpreted a pit call and stopped unnecessarily. Coulthard's decision to honour a pre-race agreement that whoever led into the second corner should win, brought him undeserved flak. Michael Schumacher suffered a mechanical failure after five laps — his only one of the year.

Pole position: Hakkinen, 1m 30.010s

Fastest lap: Hakkinen, 1m 31.649s

AUSTRALIA

In 1996 it was 'all change' for the Australian Grand Prix. Instead of finishing the season in Adelaide, the circus began the trail in Melbourne, at a new street/road course. Unlike sinuous places such as Monte Carlo, the three-mile strip around Albert Park lake is relatively wide and open, with 90-degree corners punctuating flat-out sections which give an average lap speed in excess of 130mph.

The cars are particularly spectacular through the fast left-right at Turn 11 which, surprisingly considering its high speed nature, can also represent a passing opportunity if everything is right. Other opportunities exist at the tight, slow 45mph penultimate corner, while the entry to the first corner is wide enough to encourage the adventurous. It's also tighter than it looks, as the first lap tangle between Villeneuve, Irvine and Herbert demonstrated in 1996.

Being Oz, the weather is normally fine and sunny and the biggest natural problem the drivers face is a dirty line, symptomatic of tracks which aren't normally used as racing venues. Consequently, first day times tend to be slower than usual and even less representative. Come race day, brake wear is a chief concern for the teams due to the combination of high temperatures and heavy braking into slow corners. Heinz-Harald Frentzen was robbed in 1997 when a disc exploded when he led within sight of the flag on his Williams debut. Aussie organisation is first class and it's always a fascinating race purely because it establishes the new season's pecking order.

BRAZIL

The original five-mile Interlagos used to be one of the most testing venues on the calendar. In essence, a fast outer section with a slower trip through the infield, its bumpy first corner meant that in the ground effect heyday of 1980, the drivers reported problems keeping their feet on the pedals!

Predictably, that awesome first turn now has a chicane, and although the new 2.6-mile circuit (first used in 1990) is a shadow of its former self, Interlagos is still an interesting venue.

Set in a suburb of Sao Paulo, the track seems a long way from the glorious beaches that were a feature of Rio, but drivers who have wintered on the sand rather than in the gym will soon be caught out. Unusually, Interlagos runs anti-clockwise and the g-forces impose demands on the opposite side of the neck/body. There's not too much a driver can do to simulate the effects and, together with the heat, it means the Brazilian Grand Prix often exacts a high physical toll on a driver, especially coming so early in the season.

The surface doesn't help. The organisers always claim to have done plenty of resurfacing and yet perennially the drivers speak of one thing: bumps.

The average lap speed approaches 125mph, with most of the overtaking happening into the first corner or at the end of the back straight. The uphill Juncao left-hander at the end of the lap is key to setting up an overtaking move into the first corner. The back end goes light here and can even catch out the best; remember Senna chasing Schumacher in '94? Post-Senna, the atmosphere is more subdued, but that's relative. The Brazilians love their motor racing and the circuit, set in a natural bowl, provides lots of good spectator vantage points.

Interlagos, Sao Paulo

(2.687 miles) 72 laps

LAST YEAR

After the 'gifts' at Jerez in '97 and in Australia a fortnight earlier, Mika Hakkinen took his first 'real' win. The McLarens finished 1-2 again but Michael Schumacher and Alexander Wurz at least managed to stay on the same lap. Politics ruled in the paddock with McLaren's innovative double brake system outlawed on the grounds that it was effectively four-wheel steering. Wurz pulled off a memorable move at the end of the pit straight to pass Heinz-Harald Frentzen.

Pole position: Hakkinen, 1m 17.092s

Fastest lap: Hakkinen, 1m 19.337s

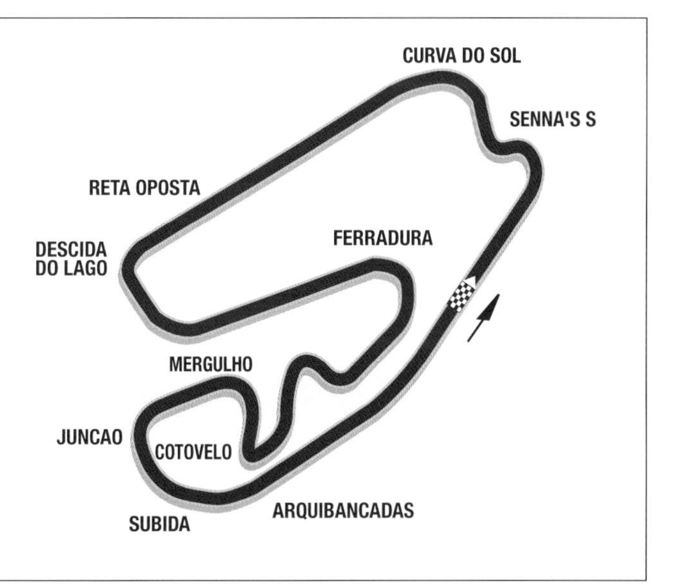

SAN MARINO

Just as Hockenheim always invokes memories of Jim Clark, so Imola will always be the place that claimed the great Ayrton Senna.

The track, set amid beautiful wooded countryside, was actually built in the fifties but did not host a Grand Prix until 1979, when Niki Lauda won a non-championship race. Italy annexed a second fully-fledged race in 1981, getting around the edict that each country should have just one race by naming the event after the tiny principality of San Marino.

Originally the track was regarded as nothing special, but as the more challenging venues gradually became sanitised by safety developments, Imola came to be regarded as one of the more testing circuits. The flat-out run down to Tosa was an overtaking site par excellence, and Tamburello, although easily flat in the lexicon of an F1 driver, was awesome nonetheless.

All that came to an end after the tragic events of 1994. First, Austrian Roland Ratzenberger crashed his Simtek fatally on the approach to Tosa during qualifying, and then Senna died in the race when his Williams left the road at Tamburello. The weekend sparked a number of safety changes and by the time the circus returned in 1995, Imola had extra chicanes before both corners.

Overtaking is now a genuine problem at Imola, but not impossible. The race is always popular with both drivers and spectators. The traditional start to the European season, many choose it to first see the new car/driver combinations.

Circuit Enzo e Dino Ferrari, Imola

(3.06 miles) 62 laps

LAST YEAR

David Coulthard scored his lone win of the year but championship leader Mika Hakkinen hit trouble when a rogue gearbox bearing halted him. Michael Schumacher finished second ahead of Ferrari team mate Eddie Irvine, with Jacques Villeneuve heading home Williams colleague Heinz-Harald Frentzen and Jean Alesi claiming the final point for Sauber.

Pole position: Coulthard, 1m 25.973s

Fastest lap: M Schumacher, 1m 29.345s

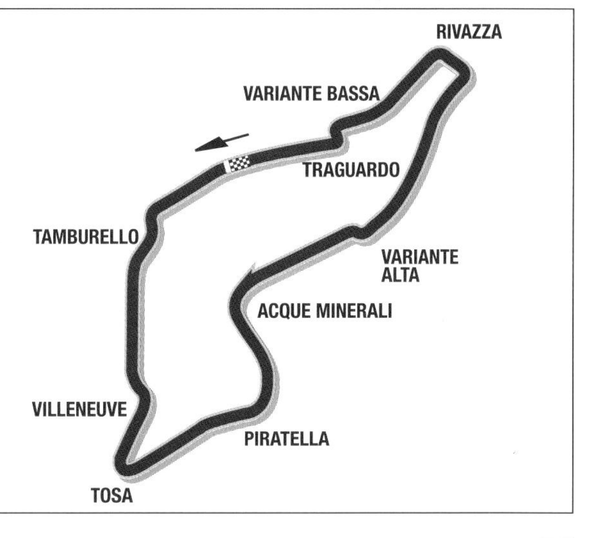

MONACO

Monaco is Formula 1's glamour shop window. Yachts bob up and down in the harbour and the race is the focal point of lavish sponsor entertainment. Many a good bash in Monte Carlo has secured next year's budget!

The race has been run since 1929 and has witnessed some great drama. Sir Jack Brabham crashed at the last corner in 1970, pressured by the chasing Jochen Rindt, and in 1981 Riccardo Patrese won as a succession of leaders, including the Italian himself, crashed, spun or ran out of fuel within sight of the flag.

Americans, to whom high speeds are all, are nonplussed to see sub 90mph average speeds, and yet any F1 fans owes himself a visit to Monaco. The race is an anachronism and if it were anywhere else would have been scratched long ago and yet it is genuinely spellbinding to witness the capabilities of a modern day F1 car in an environment where its speed and power are emphasised by the proximity of buildings.

Spectating is restricted for those without privileged access, but anyone who can beg, steal or borrow the opportunity to see a Grand Prix car exiting Casino Square, or stand in the tunnel while a car flashes by, should not pass it up. If you ever thought that drivers are overpaid, just watch them at work in Monte Carlo.

The circuit calls for absolute precision and allows the true ace to shine. Ayrton Senna was awesome here, winning six times, and Michael Schumacher is now the star. He made a faux pas on lap 1 in 1996, however, and will be out to make up for another disappointing race last year when he hit both Wurz and Diniz.

Monte Carlo, Monaco

(2.09 miles) 78 laps

LAST YEAR

Mika Hakkinen scored his fourth win in six races with a fine drive, leading all the way from pole position. Team mate David Coulthard shadowed him in the early stages before he was hit by a blown engine. Michael Schumacher, heir apparent to Ayrton Senna's 'King of Monaco' crown, had an uncharacteristic weekend, crashing in practice and hitting more trouble in the race. Giancarlo Fisichella was an impressive second, with Eddie Irvine third.

Pole position: Hakkinen, 1m 19.798s

Fastest lap: Hakkinen, 1m 22.948s

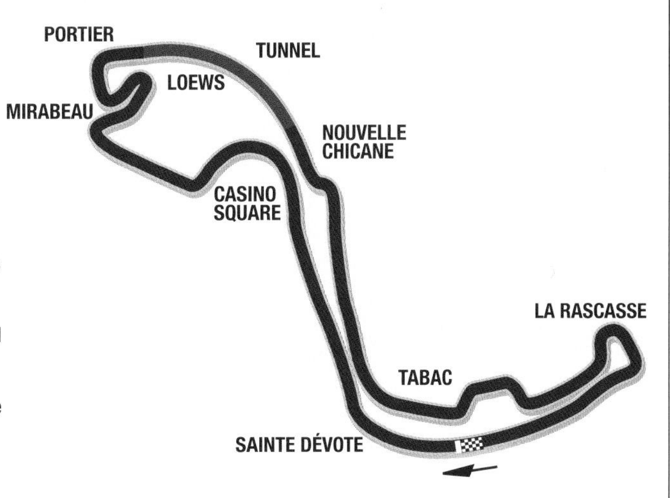

Circuit de Catalunya, Barcelona

(2.93 miles) 65 laps

LAST YEAR

Another dominant McLaren 1-2 as Mika Hakkinen headed home team mate David Coulthard with Michael Schumacher's third-placed Ferrari more than half a minute in arrears. Alexander Wurz scored another fourth place for Benetton and Rubens Barrichello was fifth in what was to be Stewart's best Grand Prix of the year. The Brazilian beat reigning champion Jacques Villeneuve's Williams into sixth.

Pole position: Hakkinen, 1m 20.262s

Fastest lap: Hakkinen, 1m 24.275s

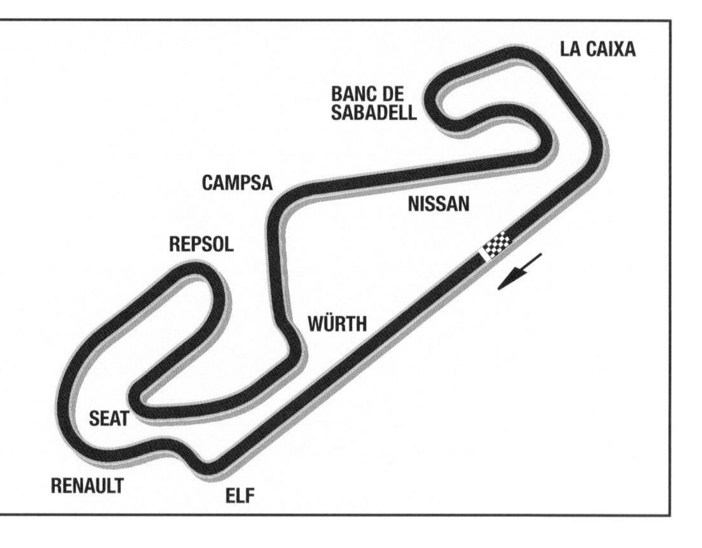

SPAIN

The Spanish Grand Prix has a long history, dating back to 1951 and a street circuit race at Pedralbes. The exciting Monjuich circuit, running up hill and down dale through a Barcelona park, saw Jackie Stewart win for Matra in 1969, while Lotus team mates Jochen Rindt and Graham Hill both crashed at the identical spot after dramatic wing failures.

A similar accident to Rolf Stommelen six years later, in which spectators were killed, brought the end of the event and a permanent move to a tight, switchback circuit at Jarama. Overtaking was nigh on impossible and Gilles Villeneuve scored a superbly controlled win there in 1981 when he held off a four-car chasing train for the entire race in an agricultural turbocharged Ferrari.

From Jarama, the race moved to Jerez in 1986 but was back in Barcelona five years later at the new purpose-built Circuit de Catalunya. The front straight is one of the longest in F1 and the image of Mansell and Senna running wheel-to-wheel down it, a cigarette paper's width apart, remains indelibly etched in the minds of most fans.

For spectators, first lap action is almost guaranteed at the sweeping first corner Elf Ess, where gravel run-off is generous. The testing fifth gear right-hander onto the straight is an important and spectacular corner, with drivers using all the kerb and more in an effort to maximise straight-line speed. The average lap speed is around 130mph, the weather is nearly always good and Barcelona, 40 minutes away, is a fine place to retire to for an evening out.

Circuit Gilles Villeneuve, Montreal

(2.74 miles) 69 laps

LAST YEAR

A race of controversy as both McLarens were out by quarter distance, Hakkinen with a gearbox problem and Coulthard with throttle trouble. Michael Schumacher took full advantage to score 10 points, but not before he had collected Heinz-Harald Frentzen's Williams as he left the pits. Schumacher was able to serve a stop-go penalty and still win. Giancarlo Fisichella finished second for Benetton with Eddie Irvine joining him on the podium once again.

Pole position: Coulthard, 1m 18.213s

Fastest lap: Schumacher, 1m 19.379s

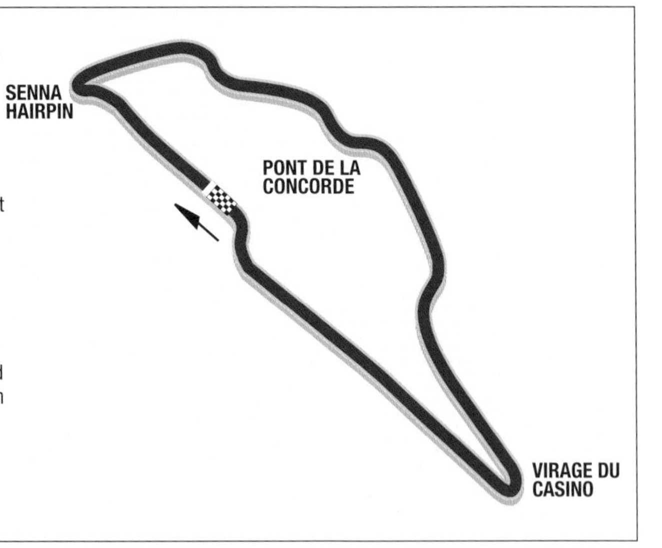

CANADA

Canada hosted its first Grand Prix in 1967, with the race originally alternating between Mosport Park and St Jovite. Both were regarded as dangerous, however, and the Canadian Grand Prix moved to a new circuit built on the site of Expo 67 at Ile Notre Dame for 1978. In a fairy tale story, local hero Gilles Villeneuve won the race in his Ferrari 312T3 — his first win — after Jean-Pierre Jarier led convincingly in a one-off appearance in the Lotus 79, the class of the field that year.

Tragedy struck in 1982 when Didier Pironi stalled his Ferrari on the pole and the unsighted rookie, Riccardo Paletti, ran into the back of him and was fatally injured.

With a fast front section running parallel to the 1976 Olympic rowing basin and a back section punctuated by chicanes and tight 90-degree corners, the track still has a 125mph average. It is one of the toughest on brakes and fuel consumption, although the latter is not such a factor since the reintroduction of refuelling to grand prix racing in 1994.

The circuit is easily reached from cosmopolitan Montreal and Canada is a popular race with drivers and spectators alike. Overtaking, once again, is difficult, with tip-toe outbraking bids into the final hairpin very much the order of the day. Another opportunity exists into the Turn 14 chicane leading onto the front straight, but is not for the faint-hearted.

Since its move from an October to June date, the cases of inclement weather turning the race into a lottery have reduced, but Montreal still seems to have the knack of turning up a surprise mid-season result.

FRANCE

The French Grand Prix has the richest history of all, with the first race run at Le Mans in 1906. Since the advent of the world championship in 1950, the event has been run at Reims, Rouen, Le Mans, Clermont Ferrand, Paul Ricard, Dijon and finally the current venue at Magny Cours in the centre of the country.

Magny Cours was developed into a Grand Prix standard track with the support of Francois Mitterand and first hosted the race in 1991. A typical modern venue, many people bad mouth Magny Cours as a boring track lacking atmosphere. When compared with the spectacle of Rouen and Clermont, that's true, but they belong to another era. There are still some interesting places to spectate.

The fast Estoril first turn dictates speed all the way down the long straight, with the best chance for overtaking coming at the end, in the braking area for the supertight 35mph Adelaide Hairpin.

The track is the smoothest on the calendar, with aerodynamics and mechanical grip at a premium around the 125mph lap. With such an emphasis on the car's capability, you can almost invariably take a look at a Magny Cours grid and note the animals going in two-by-two.

Even if the circuit doesn't grab you, this is France, the food and wine are, of course, delightful, and you can take the opportunity to stock up on the way home. Paris is a two and a half hour drive away.

Circuit de Nevers, Magny Cours

(2.64 miles) 72 laps

LAST YEAR

Ferrari scored its first 1-2 finish since 1990 as Michael Schumacher took his third win of the year and Eddie Irvine managed to hold off Hakkinen. The McLarens had made a strong getaway at the first time of asking but when Jos Verstappen's Stewart stalled on the grid, a problem with the abort procedure resulted in the race being red flagged. Ferrari took full advantage. Villeneuve was fourth, ahead of Wurz and Coulthard, who was delayed by a refuelling problem.

Pole position: Hakkinen, 1m 14.929s

Fastest lap: Coulthard, 1m 17.523s

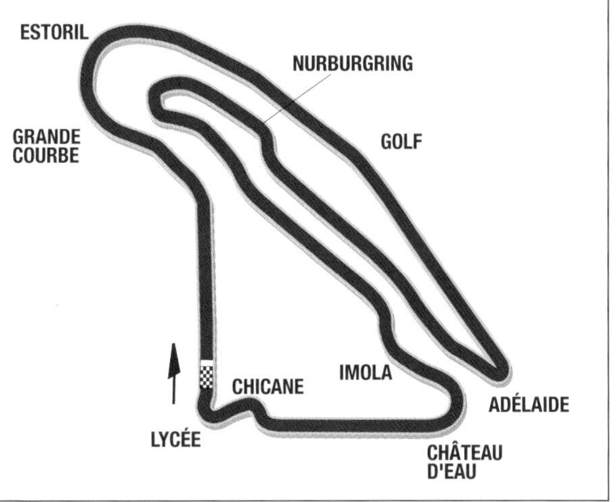

Silverstone

(3.19 miles) 60 laps

LAST YEAR
A hat-trick for Michael Schumacher brought him to within two points of Mika Hakkinen. The Finn seemed to have the rain meister handled but a Safety Car opened the race and allowed Schumacher to steal maximum points. There was more controversy as the German passed Alexander Wurz under a yellow with 17 laps to go and the stewards added a 10s penalty to his race time. The rules state that this facility exists only if the offence happens within the last 12 laps. Amid confusion, Schumacher 'took the flag' in the pits. His brother scored Jordan's first championship point of 1998.
Pole position: Hakkinen, 1m 23.271s
Fastest lap: M Schumacher, 1m 35.704s

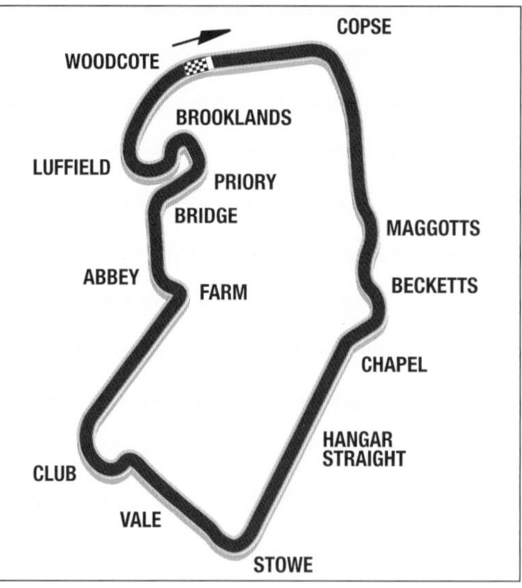

BRITAIN

Brooklands first hosted the British Grand Prix, in 1926, before a couple of races at Donington in the thirties. The home of the British Grand Prix proper, however, is Silverstone, with the race first visiting Northamptonshire in 1948, using the perimeter roads of the former airfield.

In 1950 the circuit held the very first round of the current World Championship, with victory going to Giuseppe Farina – who went on to take the inaugural championship title – in front of a watching King George VI.

After a brief spell alternating with Aintree, the British Grand Prix switched between Silverstone and Brands Hatch for over 20 years between the mid sixties and eighties. Many purists expressed a preference for the sweeps and natural amphitheatre at the Kent venue, but a five year deal with Silverstone in 1986 spelled the end of the road for Brands. Silverstone has now hosted the Grand Prix every year since 1987.

In line with recent developments, the circuit has continuously evolved and is now very different from the track on which Keke Rosberg qualified a Williams at 160mph in 1985. Landmarks such as the old Stowe, Club and Woodcote are much changed, but the circuit still represents a challenge, most notably through the Becketts sweepers and Bridge Corner. Michael Schumacher has been involved in much Silverstone controversy in recent years: the black flag disqualification in 1994, the coming-together with Hill the year after, and winning the race in the pit lane last year! A home race for 75 per cent of the F1 industry, Silverstone undoubtedly has a special feel.

As for the car parking, take a book...

AUSTRIA

The majestic Osterreichring set amid the Styrian mountains used to be one of the most intoxicating venues on the Grand Prix calendar.

The track first appeared in 1970 after the Austrian Grand Prix was first run on the unpopular Zetweg airfield six years earlier. It was the same year that Austria's Jochen Rindt became the sport's first posthumous champion, killed in a qualifying accident at Monza a month after the race in his home country. After Rindt, however, the emergence of Niki Lauda guaranteed a fervent throng of home supporters who never seemed deterred by heavy rain which perennially rolled down the hillsides and flooded the camp site.

A fatal accident to Mark Donohue in 1975 meant that a chicane was installed before the daunting blind brow Hella Licht first corner, but the track still remained devastatingly fast, with the 200mph arrival at the Bosch Kurve particularly spectacular. The thrice started race of 1987, won by Nigel Mansell, was the last Grand Prix to be held on the great circuit.

Gerhard Berger was always a prime mover behind the return of the race. Predictably, the old circuit was now politically incorrect and while the new A1-Ring may not be exactly the Osterreichring, the scenery is still straight out of the Sound of Music and the locals have Alexander Wurz to cheer. If you have time, incorporate it as a holiday with the chance to take in the culture of Vienna or Salzburg and you won't go far wrong.

A1-Ring, Spielberg

(2.68 miles) 71 laps

LAST YEAR

Qualifying was a lottery as changing weather conditions meant that whoever got a lap in latest went quickest, producing a Giancarlo Fisichella/Jean Alesi front row. Hakkinen and Schumacher started from row two but were soon at the front, the Finn scoring an accomplished win to put his title challenge back on course. Schumacher survived a grassy excursion to finish third, behind an inspired Coulthard, who charged through from 14th on the grid.

Pole position: Fisichella, 1m 29.598s
Fastest lap: Coulthard, 1m 12.878s

REMUS KURVE
GOSSER KURVE
NIKI LAUDA KURVE
JOCHEN RINDT KURVE
CASTROL KURVE
MOBILKOM KURVE

PARI
CAMPA

Hockenheim

(4.24 miles) 45 laps

LAST YEAR
On Mercedes home territory Mika Hakkinen and David Coulthard delighted the three pointed star's management by claiming the front row and dominating the race from lights to flag. Jacques Villeneuve turned in a strong drive to finish well in touch, with Damon Hill pipping the old enemy Michael Schumacher to fourth place. Brother Ralf made it two Jordans in the top six.
Pole position: Hakkinen, 1m 41.838s
Fastest lap: Coulthard, 1m 46.116s

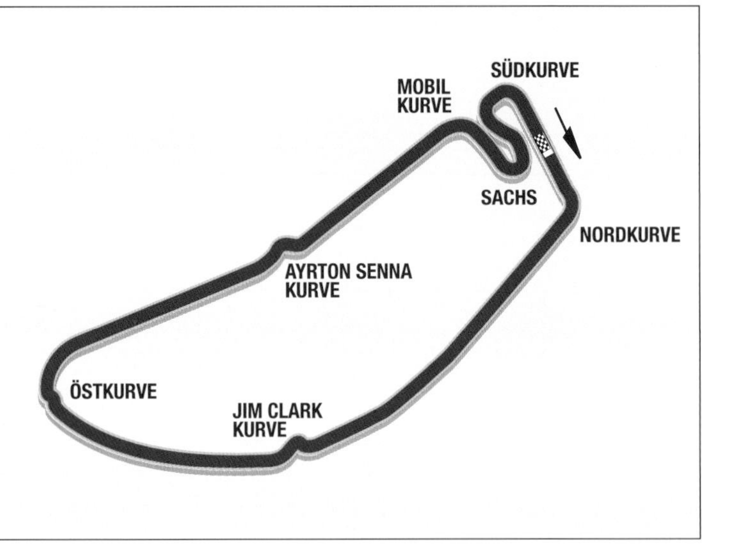

GERMANY

The German Grand Prix was first held at Avus in 1926 but its spiritual home is undoubtedly the old Nurburgring. The tortuous 14-mile ribbon was the most daunting track of them all and prompted Jackie Stewart to say: 'You always took a long, wistful look at your driveway as you left home for the 'Ring. Anyone who says he liked the place was either crazy or a liar.'

Demands for safety changes at The Ring meant that the German Grand Prix moved to Hockenheim in 1970 and when Niki Lauda's fiery crash sounded the death knell for Nurburgring in 1976, the race returned permanently to Hockenheim, notwithstanding a one-off race on an unrecognisable 'new Nurburgring' in 1984.

Hockenheim will always be the place that claimed the life of the great Jim Clark — in an F2 accident in 1968 — and was never really popular with driver or spectator. However, as more insipid venues have worked their way onto the calendar, the track has become somewhat unique and with a 145mph average lap speed it is now the fastest circuit on the grand prix schedule.

A flat-out blind punctuated by three chicanes and a tight stadium section filled with klaxon-blowing, flag-waving Schumacher fans, the place definitely has atmosphere even if spectating opportunities are limited. The circuit is all about straight-line speed and aerodynamic efficiency. The cars therefore run virtually no wing, which makes stability in the chicanes and stadium section a problem. Commitment from the driver is more vital than ever in extracting a lap time. Engines take a caning.

HUNGARY

The Hungaroring took Formula 1 behind the Iron Curtain for the first time, in 1986. Following on from Hockenheim, the track represents the other end of the scale. The low downforce settings are left at home and the cars run more wing here than at any venue other than Monaco.

The difficulty of overtaking in Hungary is well documented and was amply demonstrated by Thierry Boutsen's ability to hold off Ayrton Senna for the entire race in 1990. Nobody seemed to have told Nigel Mansell, however, the Bulldog Brit scoring one of his best ever victories in Hungary after starting his Ferrari from 12th place!

Most of the action happens at the end of the front straight, with drivers committing themselves deep into the 180 degree first turn in order to make up positions. Real opportunists also try a dive down the inside of Turn Two. Regarded as uninteresting at first, the Hungaroring definitely has something. It might not be the first choice on most people's visit list, but many who do go become committed fans. Buda and Pest, on opposite sides of the Danube, are superb places to relax and enjoy a holiday. The race's presence on the calendar, suspect at one stage, now seems guaranteed.

The average lap speed is around 115mph and the race always seems to produce some interesting strategic gambles — none more so than last year, when Michael Schumacher managed to put one across the McLarens in superb style on a three-stop strategy.

Hungaroring, Budapest

(2.46 miles) 77 laps

LAST YEAR

A superb tactical show of strength by Michael Schumacher and Ferrari technical director Ross Brawn outfumbled McLaren and put Maranello back in the championship chase. Ferrari's decision to opt for a three-stop strategy despite a delayed first stint demanded that Schumacher build up a 25 second lead in 19 laps. Coulthard, Villeneuve, Hill, Frentzen and Hakkinen took the minor places, the championship leader delayed by a handling problem.

Pole position: Hakkinen, 1m 16.973s

Fastest lap: M Schumacher, 1m 19.286s

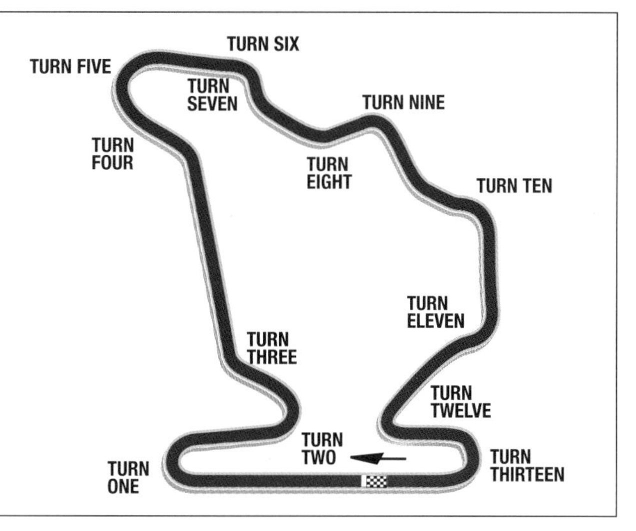

Spa-Francorchamps

(4.32 miles) 44 laps

LAST YEAR

The most dramatic race of the year. The first lap saw utter carnage as David Coulthard lost it in front of the pack on the run down to Eau Rouge. Twelve cars were eliminated but everyone escaped unscathed. At the restart Damon Hill led but Michael Schumacher passed him and romped away. He then tripped over Coulthard's McLaren while lapping it and stormed down to McLaren to vent his spleen. Eddie Jordan got his glory day as Hill and Ralf Schumacher come home first and second.

Pole position: Hakkinen, 1m 48.682s

Fastest lap: M Schumacher, 2m 03.766s

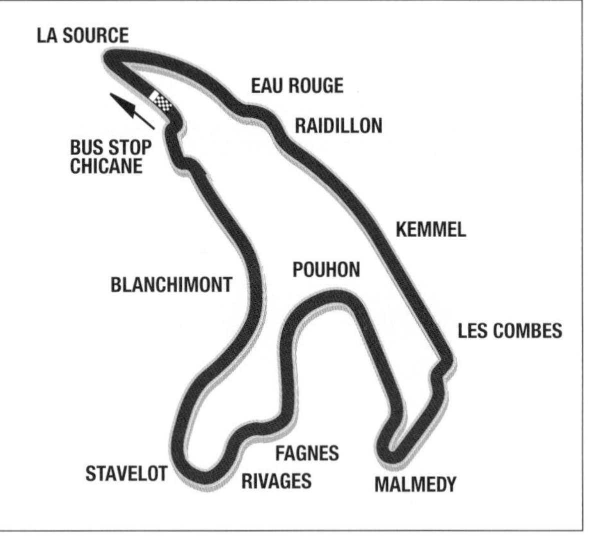

BELGIUM

The original Spa-Francorchamps was the nearest rival to the Nurburgring Nordschleife in terms of challenge to a Grand Prix driver. It first hosted the Belgian Grand Prix in 1924 and then became an established part of the official World Championship from the outset in 1950.

Located in the Belgian Ardennes, the original track was over eight miles long and incorporated some frightening high-speed road sections. The area's propensity for sudden rain meant that one part of the circuit could be bone dry while another was soaked. Such micro climate caused a multiple accident in 1966, the most serious crash of Jackie Stewart's career.

Jim Clark won the race four times but loathed the place and, in 1972, a new home was found at the supersafe Nivelles. It was unpopular, however, and the Belgian Grand Prix moved to Zolder before returning to a revised four-mile Spa in 1983. Zolder, sadly, will always be remembered as the track that claimed the great Gilles Villeneuve, Jacques's father, in a qualifying accident in 1982.

Spa is still a great challenge, probably the biggest on the modern calendar and, along with Suzuka, gets most driver votes for favourite track. The thrilling sweep through Eau Rouge was temporarily removed for 1995 as part of the safety changes made after Ayrton Senna's Imola accident the previous year, but thankfully has now returned. Every Grand Prix fan owes himself a trip to Spa. Oh, and don't miss out on the frites and mayonnaise while you're there! Schumacher is always magnificent and Damon Hill won last year for Jordan! Remember to pack a waterproof...

ITALY

Monza, built in 1922, is the undoubted home of the Italian Grand Prix, hosting the country's world championship race every year since 1950, with the exception of a one-off race at Imola in 1980.

The wide front straight is one of the most famous and instantly recognisable stretches of track anywhere and was originally combined with quite awesome banking which, today, remains in a state of decay for onlookers to marvel at. If you visit Monza, try walking up and staying upright!

The original Monza was practically flat-out all the way, incorporating great corners such as the Curva Grande, Lesmos and Parabolica. It gave rise to traditional Monza slipstreamers which were often decided by who had the tallest penultimate gear ratio for the sprint to the line out of Parabolica. Jackie Stewart won an extraordinary blanket finish in 1969, as Jochen Rindt, Bruce McLaren and Jean-Pierre Beltoise all shot across the line next to him. Two years later, Peter Gethin won the fastest Grand Prix of all time here, at 151mph. The track has always seen its fair share of drama, never more so than in 1988, when Jean-Louis Schlesser, having a one-off race for Williams, tripped up race leader Ayrton Senna, facilitating a Ferrari 1-2 just weeks after Enzo's death. It also prevented Ron Dennis and McLaren from achieving their stated aim of winning every race that year.

The fervour of the Ferrari faithful — the tifosi — gives Monza an atmosphere all its own although, ironically, three chicanes now punctuate the track and overtaking is actually regarded as difficult! Along with Hockenheim, the race represents the deepest examination of engine reliability and, coming at a crucial stage in the season, a tense race is almost inevitable.

Autodromo Nazionale di Monza, Monza

(3.58 miles) 58 laps

LAST YEAR

Michael Schumacher delighted the tifosi with pole position but it was the McLarens which set the early pace until Coulthard was sidelined by a blown engine. Schumacher and Hakkinen fought out the lead until the Finn ran out of brakes in the closing stages and was fortunate to survive a high speed spin at the Roggia chicane and get home fourth. Eddie Irvine backed up Schumacher to send the fans home in delirium after a Ferrari 1-2 saw Schumacher join Hakkinen at the head of the championship table. Ralf Schumacher was third for Jordan.

Pole position: M Schumacher, 1m 25.289s

Fastest lap: Hakkinen, 1m 25.139s

Nurburgring

(2.83 miles) 67 laps

LAST YEAR

It looked like an uphill task for Mika Hakkinen as the Ferraris qualified 1-2. The Finn's worst fears were realised when Schumacher led with Irvine riding shotgun. Undeterred, Hakkinen passed the Irishman and then 'outSchumachered' Michael to take the lead after the first pit stop. He went on to score the best win of his career at a crucial time. A disappointed Schumacher was second with David Coulthard third, ahead of Irvine, Heinz-Harald Frentzen's Williams and Giancarlo Fisichella's Benetton.

Pole position: Schumacher, 1m 18.561s

Fastest lap: Hakkinen, 1m 20.450s

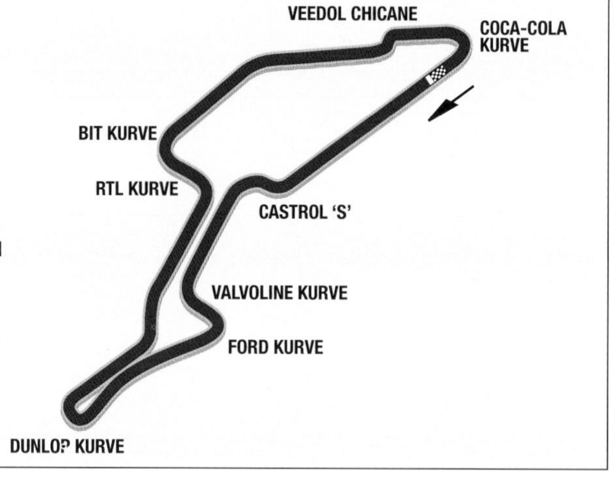

EUROPE

The success of the Schumacher brothers and a take-off in German interest all but guaranteed a second race for the country, although veiled as the 'Luxembourg' or 'European' Grand Prix. The current Nurburgring will always suffer in comparison with the dramatic Nordschleife, in whose shadow it sits, but is becoming an established year-end feature of the calendar.

No true Grand Prix fan minds visiting the Eifel mountains and, if nothing else, should be sure to pay their handful of Marks and sample the old circuit first hand. A degree of restraint will be required and a company car is preferable! And a word of warning — more weekend speedsters have met their end on the old 'Ring than have racing drivers...

The 'new Nurburgring' first hosted a Grand Prix in 1984 and, although bland, can produce an interesting race. Last year's race, indeed, was the defining point in Mika Hakkinen's championship success as he drove superbly to assert himself in his battle with Michael Schumacher, giving the Ferrari star a taste of his own medicine with a superb tactical drive.

The track now boasts an average lap speed of 130mph and, it hardly needs to be said, overtaking is difficult. Some try into the tight first corner — Ralf Schumacher famously taking off his brother on lap 1 in 1997! — while others wait for a late-braking stab into the Veedol S. The scenery is great and the autumnal weather crisp. Pack a fleece!

MALAYSIA

With Zhuhai failing to keep its early season Chinese Grand Prix date due to logistical problems, the Malaysian Grand Prix will become the first Asian venue on the F1 calendar when the circus visits in October.

The Malaysians have invested almost £50 million in what should be a medium speed venue some 45 miles south of the country's capital, Kuala Lumpur. A slow-down in the Malaysian economy has brought its own problems but work on the track went ahead, funded by the private investment company Malaysian Airport Berhad.

An impressive main grandstand dominates the main straight and the race has generated enormous interest among the locals, but whether the country's ecomomic problems will allow enough spectators through the turnstiles remains to be seen.

The Malaysian premier is hoping that the race will heighten tourist interest in the country and a 2300 acre recreation complex is planned around the track, including a golf course and a theme park. The site, formerly a rain forest, will also include top class hotels, restaurants and a shopping centre.

It is a long time since F1 commercial boss Bernie Ecclestone expressed his wish to take F1 to Asia but the plan has finally come to fruition. 'Everyone thought I was a lunatic,' Ecclestone said, 'but we are a world championship, not a European championship, and we need to have a presence in Asia.'

Drivers who have visited the track report a varied track layout with one or two distinct overtaking spots. Projected lap speed for the new layout is around 125mph.

Sepang, Kuala Lumpur

(2.09 miles) 78 laps

FIRST RACE THIS YEAR

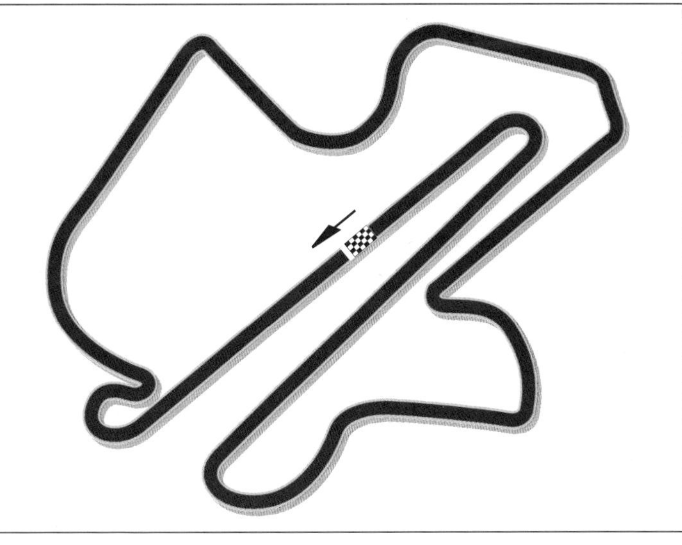

FUJI TELEVISION
FUJI-TV
FUJI-TV

JAPAN

The superb Japanese track has become an end of season fixture and is a fitting conclusion to the world championship. Other than Spa, Suzuka is regarded as the biggest test of today's Grand Prix driver.

The S curves behind the pits subject the neck to high g-loadings and one driver, making his Grand Prix debut at Suzuka, was wasted after two laps. Approaching the end of the lap, the challenging 130R corner is one of the most demanding anywhere. Although perhaps not vital to the overall lap time as it leads straight into a first gear chicane, machismo dictates that every driver wants to take it flat. Few achieve it. It was too much even for Michael Schumacher in 1991, the then rookie having an enormous accident — he discovered, years later, that he had broken his neck!

Japan played host to its first Grand Prix in 1976, at Fuji, the race settling the outcome of that season's dramatic title showdown between James Hunt and Niki Lauda. Held in streaming rain, it brought Hunt the championship after Lauda decided that conditions were too dangerous.

The race disappeared after 1977 before returning at Suzuka a decade later, coinciding with Honda's fortunes riding high. The Japanese manufacturer actually owns the track and that first race will be remembered for Nigel Mansell's practice accident which spelled the end of his championship aspirations that year. Ayrton Senna sealed his first world championship here a year later, and the race will always be remembered for those controversial incidents between Senna and Alain Prost which decided the championship in both 1989 and '90. The race might be short on history, but it's long on incident!

Suzuka

(3.64 miles) 53 laps

LAST YEAR
The championship showdown. High drama as Michael Schumacher was one of three drivers to stall on the grid. After an aborted start he was placed at the back and stormed back to third before a blown tyre — ironically, in Goodyear's last race — spelled the end of his title challenge. Hakkinen claimed the crown in fine style with his eighth win of the season. Eddie Irvine was second, ahead of David Coulthard. Damon Hill's fourth place ensured that Jordan finished fourth, ahead of Benetton in the constructors' championship.
Pole position: M Schumacher, 1m 36.293s
Fastest lap: M Schumacher, 1m 40.190s

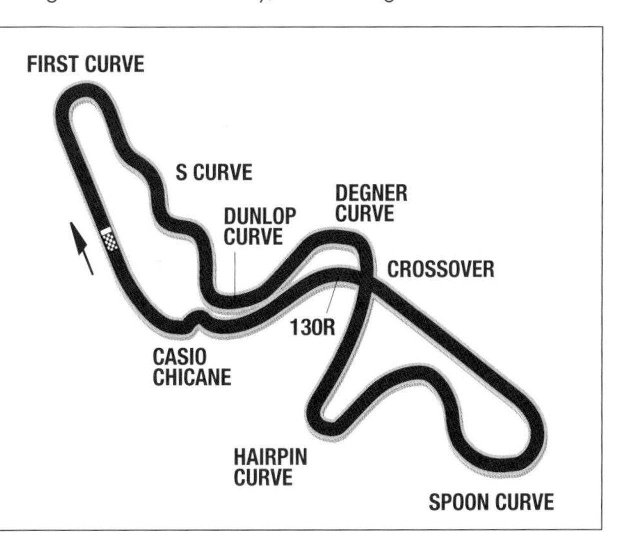

CHINA

China and Malaysia have been fighting a head-to-head battle for the honour of hosting the first Grand Prix on the Asian continent.

It looked like the Chinese had won when their race was scheduled to be the second round of the 1999 world championship, two weeks after the season-opener in Melbourne. Unfortunately for them, however, logistical problems intervened and it proved impossible to ready the track in time. The race has now been demoted to reserve status for 1999 and will be on the schedule proper come the millennium.

An FIA statement said: 'Due to the problems experienced by the organisers of the Chinese Grand Prix, the World Motor Sport Council has decided not to run the event on the date planned. It will remain as a reserve on the calendar for 1999 with a date later in the year.'

With a couple of the F1 dates provisional due to safety work or legal undertakings, however, it is still not impossible that China could host a race ahead of Malaysia's October date. The FIA has guaranteed the Chinese their place in 2000 and went on to say: 'There also remains the possibility that the FIA can secure an agreement with the teams to run an additional race. In this case, the Chinese Grand Prix could be held in the autumn of 1999.'

Zhuhai first submitted a proposal to the FIA, motor sport's governing body, in July 1995, with the idea of running the first Chinese Grand Prix in 1997. FIA president Max Mosley visited China shortly afterwards to discuss developing motor sport in the world's most highly populated country. Zhuhai has already staged GT racing in front of 100,000 spectators and the circuit was officially opened by another GT race last November.

Zhuhai Mayor Liang Guanda claims that the newly completed facility will have a capacity of

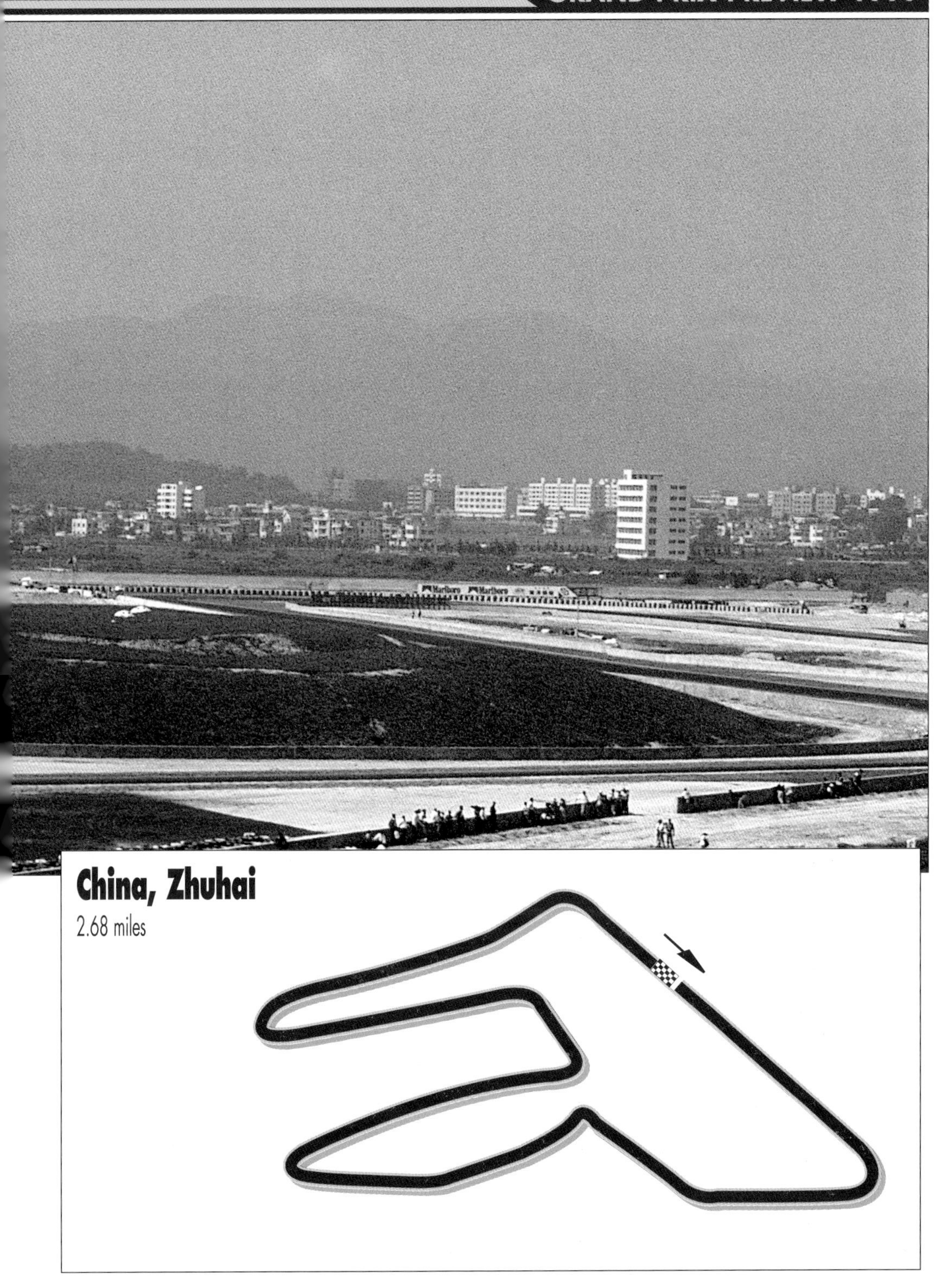

200,000 spectators, a fifth of the city's population! Jacques Villeneuve became the first F1 driver to gain experience of the track when he visited Zhuhai en route to the 1998 season finale in Japan. The 1997 world champion described the circuit as 'interesting' and complimented the Chinese on the effort being put into the new track.

WHAT IS F1 ALL ABOUT?

DANKA
DANKA
DANKA
CAMPARI
PIT LANE
PIT LANE

Key personnel

Bernie Ecclestone

Through Formula 1, Bernie Ecclestone, the son of a Suffolk trawler skipper, rose to become the highest salaried man in Britain, recently reaching number six in the Sunday Times richest 500 list.

Ecclestone raced in the fifties and owned a motorcycle dealership in Bexleyheath, Kent, where he was a close friend of Stuart Lewis-Evans, the promising Vanwall team mate to Stirling Moss and Tony Brooks. Lewis-Evans was killed at Casablanca in 1958 and Ecclestone concentrated on his business interests until returning to F1 as Jochen Rindt's manager.

In 1970, Ron Tauranac sold his interest in the Brabham team to Ecclestone and the team won championships with Nelson Piquet under Bernie's ownership.

It was managing the business affairs of Formula 1 as a whole that Ecclestone made his impression, however. Working with Max

Bernie Ecclestone is the most influential man in the sport. He has turned Formula 1 into a multi million dollar business. And he gets paid even more than Michael...

Mosley, he started to represent the affairs of the F1 constructors in negotiations with circuits, television companies, etc.

Ecclestone took Formula 1 and converted it from a haphazardly run minor sport into one of the most visible international sporting extravaganzas on earth. The global nature of F1 has always been attractive to tobacco sponsors since the beginning of commercialism in the late sixties. The other great source of income, vastly increased in recent years, is television. Having manoeuvred himself into position as the commercial rights holder, Ecclestone has skilfully exploited the potential to make both himself and F1's high fliers very rich.

Max Mosley has a legal background and has shrewdly steered the sport since taking over as FIA president.

Max Mosley

Born in 1940, the younger son of Sir Oswald Mosley via his second marriage to Diana Mitford, FIA president Max Mosley has over 30 years' experience of motor sport.

Mosley was secretary of the Oxford Union, studied physics and specialised in patent and trademark law before getting himself involved in motor racing. He raced at Formula 2 level before becoming the 'M' in the newly founded March company.

In the early days Mosley listened with disbelief to the ramblings of the Grand Prix Constructors and Entrants Association and determined to do something about it. A year or so later, when Bernie Ecclestone bought Brabham, the pair soon got together and were rapidly doing everything for the GPCA, which ultimately spawned FOCA.

With Ecclestone's negotiating skills and Mosley's legal background they made a formidable team. By the end of the seventies, when a FISA v FOCA war threatened the entire fabric of the sport, it was Mosley who thrashed out the Concorde Agreement which became the

basis of peace.

In the ultimate poacher turned gamekeeper scenario, Mosley challenged dictatorial Frenchman Jean-Marie Balestre for the presidency of FISA, the sport's governing body, in the autumn of 1991. With Ecclestone installed as vice-president (promotional affairs), suddenly they were The Establishment.

Mosley steered Formula 1 through a tricky period which followed the death of Ayrton Senna at Imola. He presents an urbane, mild mannered approach but has inner steel and is as shrewd, articulate and persuasive as any politician in Whitehall or Brussels.

Sid Watkins has been a comforting presence on the F1 scene for over 20 years.

Professor Sid Watkins

'The Prof' is a familiar sight around the Grand Prix circuits of the world. He has been Formula 1's on-track surgeon for 20 years.

Sid Watkins qualified at Liverpool University Medical School and trained as a neurosurgeon at the Radcliffe Infirmary, Oxford.

Appointed Professor of Neurosurgery in New York in the 1960s, Sid returned to the UK in the seventies to become the first holder of a similar post at the London Hospital.

His interest in cars dates back to his childhood in Liverpool, where the family owned a bike shop and garage. While in Oxford he made regular trips to Silverstone and while in the States he worked at Watkins Glen, which led to an invitation to join the RAC medical panel in 1970.

In 1978 Bernie Ecclestone asked Watkins to be responsible for medical care at all Grands Prix. When Sid travelled to Sweden, he was surprised to find that the medical centre was a caravan! He expected efficiency from the Germans but discovered a converted single decker bus. It had resuscitation and ventilation facilities but there was no anaesthetist and the

medical crew camped, slept and cooked alongside the bus, parked in the paddock. Things have changed...

Watkins has an irreverent sense of humour, likes a smoke and a glass of red wine or three, and his presence has become a source of great assurance to more than one generation of drivers. An excellent chase car system has ensured that Sid can be at any accident within seconds of its occurrence.

Formerly Brabham's chief mechanic, Charlie Whiting has a lot to think about.

Charlie Whiting

Charlie Whiting has been around motor racing for as long as Bernie Ecclestone and Max Mosley. Formerly chief mechanic at Brabham when Ecclestone was team owner, Whiting is therefore ideally placed to help police the sport.

As FIA technical delegate, it was Whiting's task to co-ordinate event scrutineering and ensure the technical compliance of competing cars. As ever advancing technology became increasingly complex, however, so Charlie's role became more and more difficult. Just as racing car design is no longer a one-man field, so the FIA had to employ outside experts in order to control the sport effectively.

A good example of this was the computerised control systems which started to dominate Formula 1 in the early nineties. With many leading designers voicing the opinion that the FIA could not police such things as traction control effectively, the governing body responded by employing the likes of LDRA (Liverpool Data Research Associates) to analyse on-board software.

Mosley's dictate that if teams were contemplating a grey area, they were to seek clarification from the FIA technical department, whose ruling would be circulated, further increased pressure on Whiting who, many agreed, had perhaps the most unenviable task in the entire pit lane.

While still overseeing technical matters, Whiting is now also the Race Director, making such decisions as when to deploy the Safety Car or stop a race.

The anatomy of an F1 team

Grand Prix racing has undergone a fundamental change since the days when many of today's leading lights first became involved.

'Sir Frank' Williams started off in the sport by brokering spare parts around the international F3 scene and adding on a healthy commission. His early days as a constructor involved conducting business from the local telephone box as finances became a little stretched. The knighthood was a long way off! But, when Frank first moved into F1 in the late sixties, you could still buy an off-the-shelf Cosworth DFV, install it in a customer chassis and go racing.

March was another example. Oxford University pals Robin Herd and Max Mosley were prime movers behind an ambitious new team which built its own car and, unbelievably,

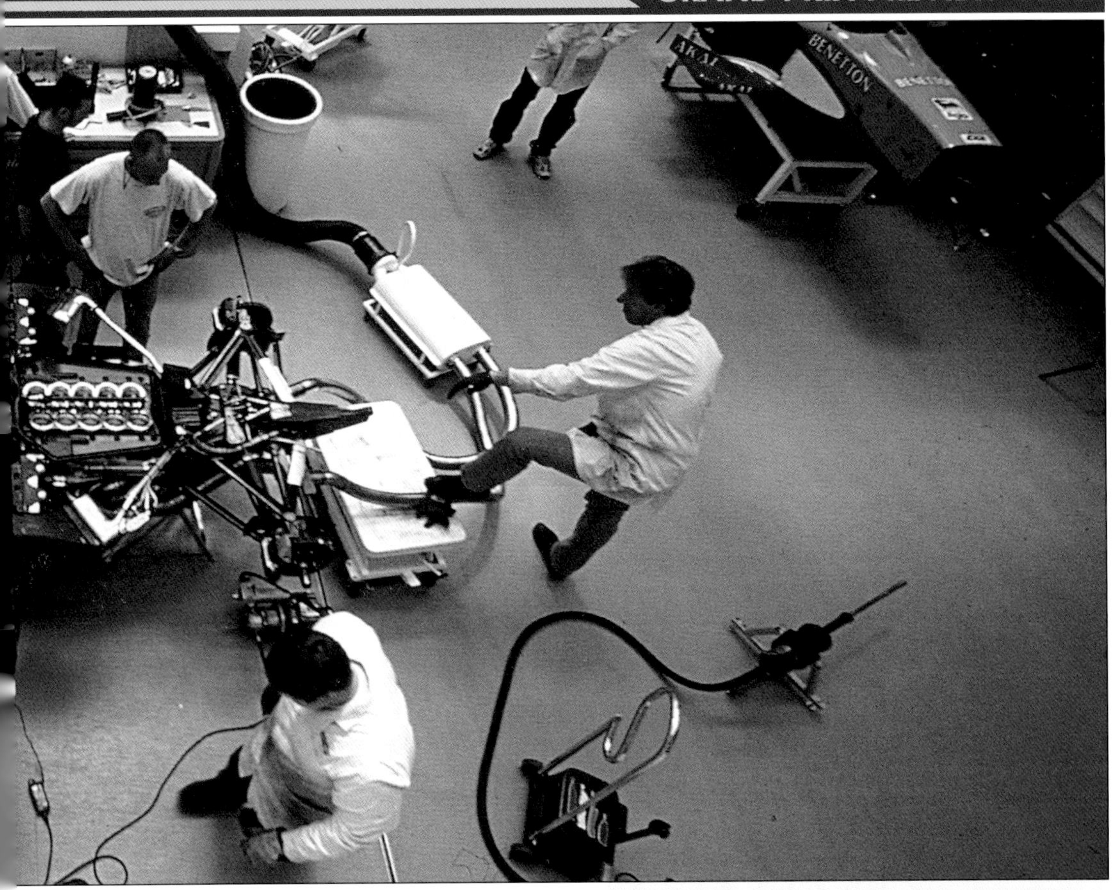

came into F1 in 1970 with reigning world champion Jackie Stewart driving.

Sound familiar? History has a habit of repeating itself and almost 30 years on, British American Racing burst onto the scene with reigning champion Jacques Villeneuve. But there the similarity ends. March's arrival just happened to coincide with Matra, for whom Stewart and Ken Tyrrell had just won the championship, wanting to run its own engine. Stewart and Tyrrell didn't fancy a Matra V12, so were suddenly in need of a chassis. March fitted the bill.

By contrast, British American Racing may have come to fruition in little over a year, but at the time of its January 6 launch, the team already boasted 202 employees. That is 100 or so fewer than the likes of Williams and Benetton and will assuredly grow.

It is now impossible to be competitive in Formula 1 without a major manufacturer engine partner. Among the top teams, Ferrari is alone in building both chassis and engine. McLaren uses Mercedes engines but the Stuttgart manufacturer calls upon the racing expertise of

Grand Prix teams do varying amounts in-house. Larger ones like Benetton employ 300 people. Below: Mercedes' yearly investment in its engine programme is estimated to be £30 million.

While the drivers are the focus of attention during a Grand Prix weekend, there are plenty of unsung heroes working behind the scenes for a team like Williams.

specialist Northamptonshire engine builder Ilmor Engineering. Some estimate that Mercedes' yearly investment in its engine programme is £30 million.

Williams and Benetton used Renault engines until the French manufacturer withdrew at the end of 1997. The V10 had won the championship five times in six years and servicing work was taken on by specialist engine builder Mecachrome. It is a revised version of this engine which will be known as a Supertec and raced by Williams, Benetton and British American Racing in 1999. These, however, are paid supply deals rather than works involvement and it is debatable whether such arrangements will facilitate an engine comparable with the very best. Just as McLaren has a partnership with Mercedes, so Williams has a new partnership with rivals BMW which sees the Munich marque back on the F1 grid in time for the new millennium.

Prost Grand Prix has a partnership with Peugeot but was hamstrung by a poor chassis in 1998 and undoubtedly has the potential to develop with John Barnard in the role of design consultant. Ford, too, has invested strongly by buying the Cosworth racing division and producing an all new V10 for 1999.

The combination of manufacturer engine partnerships allied to strong sponsorship, usually from tobacco companies, allowed the top teams to develop at great pace in the eighties. Design departments grew and teams even started to construct their own wind tunnels with aerodynamic experts as leading members of the research and development staff. Consequently, it became very difficult for smaller teams to compete, illustrated by the mid nineties demise of Lotus along with new teams such as Simtek and Pacific, which both crashed with debts of over £6 million.

Never has the concept of the rich getting richer been more apt than when applied to F1. From 1989 until 1997 inclusive, Williams, McLaren, Ferrari and Benetton monopolised the top four positions in the constructors championship, becoming universally known as 'The Big Four'. The stranglehold was finally broken in the last race of 1998 when Damon Hill's fourth place was enough to move Jordan up into the top four at the expense of Benetton.

Grand Prix team owners all talk about having 'the right package', by which they mean chassis, engine, driver, tyres and budget. If just one is missing, the team will not win. The problem facing any new team is that it is almost impossible to come in at a competitive level although that final factor — budget — can go a long way to solving the problem, as BAR intends to prove.

Stewart Grand Prix, for example, arrived in 1997 with an impeccable record in the junior formulae. Suddenly, though, they were a manufacturing business rather than merely a racing team. Such things take time to establish and it is only now that they can truly be regarded as soundly enough based to mount a challenge. A bespoke 80,000 square foot factory, which the team moved into in 1998, will undoubtedly help.

For British American Racing, the situation is slightly different. With Reynard as technical partners, the team has 20 years of manufacturing experience to call upon and a strong enough budget to attract front line drivers. Although lacking a manufacturer engine deal, the Supertec engine is based on that which won the championship five times between 1992 and 1997 and should ensure reliability. Podium positions if not outright wins should therefore be a realistic target.

The more success a team has, the greater the rewards, both in terms of prize money and potential sponsorship income. No sooner had Jordan bridged the gap between minnow and top four contender than Eddie Jordan sold a large stake to a City investment company. The business is lucrative! Jordan did it with a team perhaps half the size of his major rivals. It was structured as follows:

Jordan Grand Prix staffing levels for 1998

Department	Staff	Department	Staff
Race Team	23	Wind Tunnel	4
Composites	17	Hydraulics	4
Drawing Office	16	Production Control	4
Sub Assembly	11	Inspection	4
Commercial Department	11	Financial Department	4
Test Team	7	Machine Shop	4
Electronics/Software	7	Factory Management	3
Stores	6	Information Technology	3
Model Shop	6	Purchasing	2
Fabrication	5	Pattern Shop	2
Research & Development	4	Reception	1

How a car is made

For a new team like British American Racing it's clear cut — the BAR-Supertec 01 began with a clean sheet of paper. Or, more accurately, a blank CAD (Computer Aided Design) screen.

For just about everyone else, the F1 design game is a process of evolution. McLaren and former Williams design ace Adrian Newey is one of the most coveted men in the paddock and, as he says: 'If you're going for a clean sheet of paper these days, you have to have a damned good reason. Cars tend to develop throughout the season, so there's less of a step from one year to the next.'

The creation of a new Grand Prix car begins once any technical changes for the following

The computer screen has replaced the drawing board in design offices.

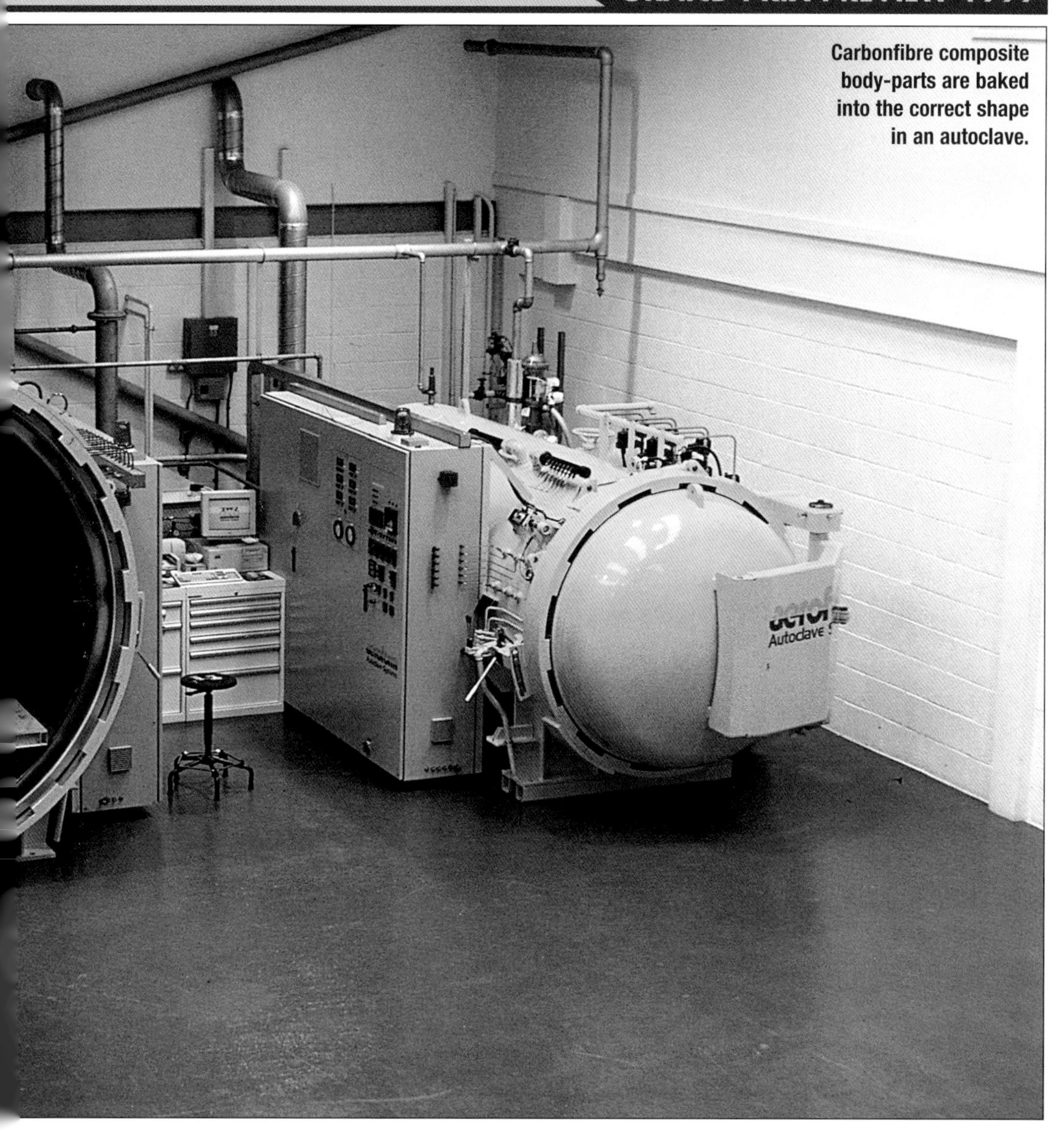

Carbonfibre composite body-parts are baked into the correct shape in an autoclave.

year have been finalised, although the designers will already have a good idea of what is coming and also what changes they want to make to their existing car.

'You develop the main theme of a new car by asking the question: how can we build a better car in ways that aren't merely modifications of the existing one? It's a matter of looking at any mechanical shortfalls and working out different chassis shapes in the wind tunnel.

'The process tends to be driven by the aerodynamic schedule and we like to be working on that by June or July. At first, you concentrate on more radical things, which might find their way onto the car in watered down form. It's actually quite difficult to evaluate new ideas. The overall effect may be worse because you haven't designed the rest of the car to allow for them.'

> *The process tends to be driven by the aerodynamic schedule*

Once the general concept is decided, the emphasis moves to those areas of the car with the longest lead times — the chassis and

'Occasionally you do get the odd light bulb idea but 90 per cent of them don't work'

Adrian Newey

Adrian Newey's designs have made a huge impact on F1 ever since his work at March. The success of McLaren (below) in 1998 has been the highlight of his career.

gearbox/rear suspension. Sidepods and wings come next.

Designers estimate that building the chassis takes approximately four months. It moves from the design department into the drawing office to be fully surfaced and drawn, going on to be machined, moulded and then actually manufactured.

After that, the designer will move on to items such as engine covers. Drawing them will take a couple of weeks, then a further week to make the pattern, a week to make the mould and then a few days to actually manufacture the part.

While the critical chassis and gearbox parts are being manufactured, the design department will keep on top of details such as brackets and wiring looms so that time is not wasted when the major components are ready.

Some of the smaller teams might contract out their chassis construction but most have their own autoclaves in which the carbon composite tubs are baked. Once all the components are together, the complete car is assembled and the team can prepare for its shakedown test.

Very occasionally, a new design concept will turn a car into a world-beater. In the late seventies, for instance, Lotus mastered ground effect, which made the Type 79 invincible.

Mario Andretti won the world championship, admirably backed up by team mate Ronnie Peterson, who sadly succumbed to injuries after a startline accident at Monza.

In 1992, Williams was the only team to race with active suspension on its FW14B. The car was already a fine design, but with the computer controlled suspension system optimising the aerodynamics, Nigel Mansell strolled to the championship practically unopposed, with team mate Riccardo Patrese runner-up.

Very occasionally a new design concept will turn a car into a world-beater

That said, the idea of the boffin with his pencil and pad, searching for inspiration, is outmoded. 'A car today is the culmination of much research,' Newey says. 'Occasionally you do get the odd light bulb idea but 90 per cent of them don't work. Most of it is relatively unexciting detailed development and hard work. Theoretically, given the research we do in the wind tunnel and on the suspension rig, if the design looks good on paper, it will be.'

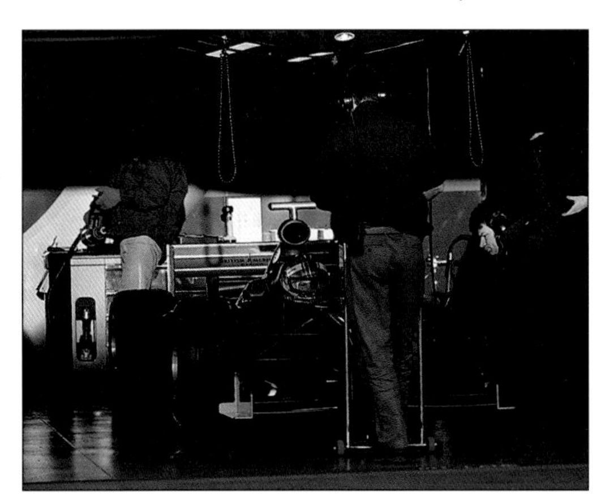

Cars in a class of their own — the active Williams FW14B of 1992 (above) and the ground effect Lotus 79 with which Mario Andretti and Ronnie Peterson dominated 1978.

As Jacques Villeneuve said at the BAR launch: 'If you've been with a team for three years, much of what goes on is just evolution. It's actually difficult to try new ideas and that is one of the exciting things about starting afresh with British American Racing.'

Although the first run on December 15 will undoubtedly have been a time of butterflies for design chief Malcolm Oastler, Newey and his rivals have a pretty good idea of what to expect when their new creations first see a race track.

'There's always a bit of a worry with a first test,' Newey says, 'just in case it turns out to be a dog for some reason, but it really should follow pretty closely what you've seen on paper and in the wind tunnel.'

Two jumbos' worth of intercontinental freight!

Moving the circus

No, not a Schuey overtaking move...cars are stacked high in the plane's hold.

As sports go, Formula 1 taxes the brains of logistics men like nothing else.

Take football. You tune in, see the 22 players and so long as the referee has remembered the ball, you're in business. With Grand Prix racing it's not quite that simple. When you next see a grid full of pristine cars, spare a thought for those responsible for getting them there, whether it be Melbourne, Monte Carlo or Montreal.

For F1 team managers, the longhaul 'flyaway' races are the biggest nightmare. All F1 freight is transported by FOCA in specially chartered Boeing 747s. At the start of a new season, when production schedules have been especially tight, it's always a race to get new cars finished off and onto the Stansted flight to Melbourne. Almost inevitably you will see some poor unfortunate arguing at a Heathrow check-in desk a few days later. His problem? The BA girl is not convinced that 60 kilos of gearbox components constitutes hand luggage!

Typically, a team packs up its equipment in special crates, notarises the contents, applies a lead seal and delivers it to Stansted airport. From there, FOCA takes over.

The cars themselves are shrink-wrapped for the journey and some 12 tonnes of spares will go in 60 lightweight boxes. FOCA imposes a weight limit of 600 kilos per car. The cars race at 500 kilos, so most teams put a box known as 'the coffin' in the cockpit, fill it up to 600 kilos and put the lid on. The cars are rolled into special aluminium pallets and stacked four high. Two 747s swallow the entire F1 circus. See it and you don't believe it will ever fly.

The longhaul 'flyaway' races are the biggest nightmare

Steve Nielsen has plenty of experience, having previously organised the transport logistics for Tyrrell.

'The sheer number of parts can cause a bit of a headache,' he says. 'If the trip involves two races at wildly different circuits, for example, you have to take double the gear ratios. One year we did Adelaide and two Japanese races — Suzuka and Aida — in the same trip. We needed 15 rear wings. It was a massive amount of freight.'

Once the teams have delivered their cargo to Stansted, FOCA takes over and ensures it gets to the circuit.

You would expect a number of nightmare tales as time goes by but, by and large, the process is drama free. The teams turn up at the circuit to find that FOCA has cleared customs and their freight is in situ.

Williams has been known to forget its tyre warmers and McLaren its pit wall TVs, but nobody has been deeply embarrassed. 'Tyrrell did actually send an empty crate to Brazil one year,' Nielsen admits. 'We had a load of them in the factory yard and an empty one got

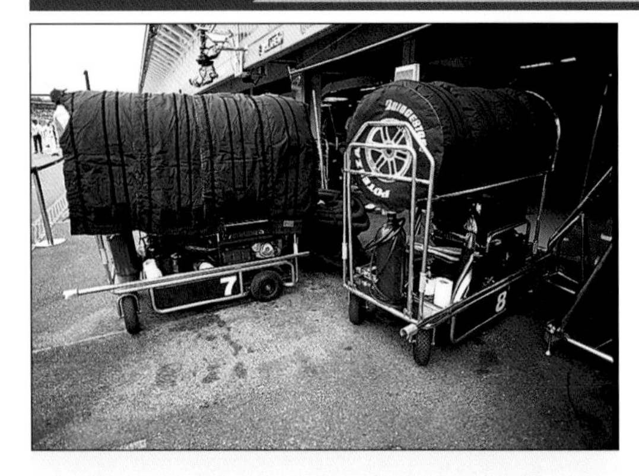

A pit needs proper organisation. Many truckers double as tyre men and are responsible for collecting and stacking the team's allocated rubber.

fork-lifted onto the lorry for Stansted. When we got to Sao Paulo we went through agonies wondering what should have been in it. If you've forgotten car parts you're in deep trouble. You can't just nip down to the local Halfords!'

The top 10 teams in the constructors' championship are given special deals for a certain amount of freight. There is a tier of discounted rates above that and then it's standard freight costs. A flyaway race will cost a mid grid team £20,000 in transportation costs before it has even turned a wheel.

'I can't tell you the hours I work because I don't think it's legal

For the European season the teams transport their cars and spares in specially built top of the range trucks which typically weigh 35—40 tonnes fully laden and are powered by 17-litre V8s pushing out almost 550bhp.

Each team will have three or four trucks which often leave on the Sunday or Monday prior to a race, to arrive by Tuesday evening or early

Custom-built trucks are the nucleus of a Grand Prix team's operation while at a European race. Below: An F1 paddock can resemble a lorry park, except that each state-of-the-art rig is pristine.

Wednesday. The trucks will then unload the cars and set up the garage in time for the race team's arrival on Thursday.

The Grand Prix paddock is all about presentation and upon arrival all team trucks will be washed down and polished by the crew, right down to having the tyres blacked and the logos picked out in white.

Many of the truckies also double as tyre men, unloading the team's wheel rims on arrival and taking them down to the tyre suppliers to have the rubber mounted. Others will also look after the fuel and possibly even the drivers' crash helmets and racing kit.

After the race, the team strips down the garage, packs up and the drivers are in action again. While there might be breathing space for some, not for a truckie. The sooner he gets back to base with the race cars, the sooner they can be stripped down and rebuilt ready for the whole process to start over again. With a race every two weeks once the season is in full swing, there is seldom time to rest.

Says one seasoned F1 truckie: 'I can't tell you the hours I work because I don't think it's legal. Twelve hour days are average, 15 hours are acceptable and 20 can sometimes be the norm. Testing is worse than racing. Sometimes the cars run to 6.30pm and then you've got to do a day's work.'

The Safety Car is used to neutralise a dangerous situation in a race without the need for a stoppage and a restart.

Safety

Paddock people fond of reminiscing speak of the days when sex was safe and motor racing dangerous. In the fifties, 21 F1 drivers lost their lives. In the sixties, the figure rose to 27. As we move toward the new millennium, it is hopefully not tempting fate to report that in the nineties the sport has claimed just two lives.

Advances in safety fuel cells allied to the crash

Mika Salo is helped away after his attempt to take Eau Rouge flat did not come off. According to Prof Watkins, the work on head padding in the cockpit area was instrumental in allowing the Finn to escape with just a headache.

sustaining properties of carbon composites have made F1 many times less perilous than once it was, but the 1994 season served as a cruel reminder that it can never be 100 per cent safe.

When Ayrton Senna was killed at Imola on May 1, it was possibly the most high profile death since JFK. The shock waves transcending the sport brought to mind Jim Clark's fatal accident at Hockenheim in April 1968. Today, though, we live in times of media saturation. The death of the world's most high profile sportsman in living rooms around the globe on prime time television presented problems for Formula 1.

The popular Roland Ratzenberger had died the previous day in circumstances just as tragic, but Senna was an icon. Brazil declared three days of national mourning. When Karl Wendlinger crashed in practice at Monte Carlo 10 days later and was hospitalised in a coma, FIA president Max Mosley knew that he had to be seen to act. Questions were being raised at governmental level and so the FIA pushed through a range of technical changes to the cars, to be introduced stage-by-stage, which addressed the safety issue by cutting downforce and reducing cornering speeds.

Questions were being raised at governmental level

Without a doubt, the two greatest advances in driver safety have been the virtual elimination of the fire risk and the protection afforded by the

Monza was once famous for its annual slipstreaming race, but in an attempt to reduce speeds it is now punctuated by three chicanes.

strong space age carbon monocoques.

In days gone by the driver literally sat amid a fuel bath, with tanks behind him and on either side. The only protection was easily punctured thin gauge sheet metal. Preoccupation with safety was regarded as somewhat sissy in the days when those magnificent men did battle with each other in linen helmets between unprotected trees!

Jackie Stewart was a leading mover in attempting to eliminate unnecessary risk as the sixties drew to a close. Fire was still the driver's number one foe until McLaren produced a carbon chassis at the beginning of the eighties. Other teams followed suit and it was not long before the regulations demanded a centrally situated fuel tank situated amidships, behind the driver, constructed from puncture-proof Kevlar and surrounded by crushable structures.

The carbon 'tubs' also proved tremendously resistant to impact without deformation, representing a great leap forward from the safety standards previously afforded by spaceframe tubing or aluminium monocoques. The greatest dangers were now the forces transmitted to the driver's body rather than absorbed by the car, and flying debris, factors which proved fatal in the Ratzenberger and Senna accidents.

Serious attention has been paid to the cockpit and steering wheel areas. In 1993, Alessandro Zanardi survived a big accident at Spa's Eau Rouge in which he hit his head on the steering wheel. Mika Hakkinen suffered similarly in his near fatal accident at Adelaide in 1995. Attention had already been paid to the cockpit sides and rear head pad after Wendlinger's accident in 1994, but it was now identified that seat-belt 'give' was allowing the driver to come forward against the dashboard area. The wearing of 75mm minimum thickness shoulder straps became mandatory and McLaren rapidly introduced a padded steering wheel. Research into rapid-fire airbags is also ongoing.

Forgetting the driver for a moment, spectator safety is even more important to the sport's governing body. Motor racing was banned in

Carbon fibre tubs can sustain very severe accidents while still affording the driver a high level of protection.

Mika Hakkinen hit his head on the steering wheel when he crashed at Adelaide in 1995. Below: Latter day McLarens are fitted with a padded wheel.

several countries following the Le Mans disaster of 1955 when Pierre Levegh's Mercedes went into the crowd. It is hard to imagine the furore that such an occurrence would cause in the politically correct nineties. The one simple law of physics, oft quoted by Mosley, is that the force of an impact increases with speed. Speed, therefore, must be contained, particularly if current circuits are not to become obsolete.

Mosley saw the need to tackle the problem at source

Many of the world's most challenging circuits from yesteryear are now just that. The Nurburgring Nordschleife, Grandaddy to them all, last hosted a Grand Prix in 1976. Of the circuits left, Spa and Suzuka are widely regarded by drivers as the most challenging.

Many purists lament 'chicane blight' which seems to have broken out everywhere in an attempt to control speeds. Monza, once famous for its annual slipstreamer, is now punctuated by three chicanes. Imola's Tamburello and Tosa — the sites of the fatal 1994 accidents — now both have chicanes.

Mosley also saw the need to tackle the problem at source. Cornering speed, he argues, is a direct function of grip and the best way to attack that is via contact patch — the tyres. By introducing longitudinal grooves into slick racing tyres for 1998, he aimed to reduce the amount of tread in contact with the road by around 17 per cent. When a Goodyear/Bridgestone tyre war brought softer compounds which all but clawed back the deficit in grip, Mosley demanded that an additional groove be cut for 1999.

Detractors sometimes accuse Formula 1 of being wise after the event but, logically, the sensible way forward is to analyse the circumstances of serious accidents and attempt to take safeguards. This has been done in almost every area. Formula 1 cars now carry data recorders, for instance.

On a personal level, safety clothing is mandatory and drivers wear fire resistant Nomex overalls, with underwear, balaclavas, socks and gloves made of similar material. Nothing can offer complete protection but modern overalls are capable of withstanding a fuel fire, which burns at almost 800 degrees centigrade, for around half a minute. Helmet visors are capable of withstanding a shotgun blast. The sport is safer than ever and those responsible can feel justifiably proud although never complacent. New for 1999 will be a mandatory safety seat developed by Stewart sponsor Lear, designed to enable the removal of an injured driver while still in place in his seat, thereby reducing the risk of aggravating any spinal injury.

Rules and regulations

Grand Prix racing is governed by an extensive set of technical and sporting regulations.

The technical regulations are highly specific and explain why the appearance of rival cars is so similar. Among the most fundamental, cars must weigh no less than 600kg, inclusive of the driver in full racing kit.

Normally aspirated engines must not exceed 3.0 litres and the overall width of the car, including the wheels, must not exceed 180cm. This maximum width was reduced for the 1998 season to restrict the ability of the car underbody to generate downforce, thereby limiting cornering speed. This requirement came hand-in-hand with the introduction of grooved tyres to limit grip. Three longitudinal grooves were required in the front tyres, with four at the rear. Grooves have to be at least 14mm wide at the contact surface and at least 2.5mm deep. For 1999, a fourth groove is required at the front. The maximum wheel width is set at 380mm.

The size of aerodynamic wings, together with their overhang, is also restricted. All cars are subject to scrutineering, during which a template is used, between 10:00 and 18:00 on the Thursday before a Grand Prix meeting starts.

Some of the key sporting rules governing F1 are:

The race length is the number of laps equal to 200 miles

- The driver must drive the car alone and unaided. It is under this rule that the FIA would outlaw any perceived driver aid.
- The race length is the number of laps equal to 200 miles (305km). However, if two hours elapse before it is reached, the leader will be shown the chequered flag at the end of the lap on which two hours is up.
- The maximum number of events in the championship is 17, the minimum eight.
- In the final race of 1997, three drivers set the identical fastest qualifying time. The better starting position went to the driver setting the time first. In the unlikely event of a dead heat

New for '99 is an extra groove in the front tyre, aimed at reducing grip and slowing speeds.

Bridgestone has to be prepared to supply the whole field if it is the only manufacturer active in Formula 1.

in the race, prizes and points for the positions involved are added together and shared equally. Hence, drivers tying for first place would score eight points each.

- Points are scored 10-6-4-3-2-1 to the first six finishers, with every race counting towards

the championship. The scores recorded by both team cars count towards the constructors' championship.

- If the make of the chassis is not the same as the engine, the title goes to the former, which shall always precede the latter in the name of the car. Hence, you can have a McLaren Mercedes but not a Mercedes McLaren.
- A fee of 2500 Swiss Francs (around £1000) must accompany any protest made.
- During a season, a team is permitted one driver change for its first car and is allowed three drivers in its second car, who may be changed at any time. After 18.00 on the day of scrutineering, a change may only be made with the consent of the stewards. Any new driver is eligible to score points in the championship.
- Testing is prohibited on any circuit during the seven days preceding a race day, except for a shakedown which must not exceed 50km. No testing is allowed on any circuit which will host a Grand Prix during the championship year, other than those hosting the British, French, Italian and Spanish Grands Prix.
- If one tyre supplier is present in the championship, it must equip all of the teams entered on ordinary commercial terms. If two companies are present they must be prepared to equip 60 per cent of the entered teams if called upon to do so. If three companies are present, 40 per cent.
- No signal of any kind may pass between a

A stop-go penalty — the accepted way of dealing with minor indiscretions.

moving car and anyone connected with it, except: legible messages on a pit board; body movement by the driver; telemetry signals from the car to the pits; lap trigger signals from pits to the car; verbal radio communication.

- Each car must be fitted with an accident data recorder.
- Spare cars may not be used in free practice but may be used for qualifying.
- A driver who abandons a car must leave it in neutral or with the clutch disengaged and with the steering wheel in place.
- Oil replenishment during a race is forbidden. All orifices for oil filling must be designed in such a way that the scrutineers can seal them.
- No one except the driver may touch a stopped car unless it is in the pits or on the starting grid.
- At no time may a car be reversed in the pit lane under its own power.

At no time may a car be reversed in the pit lane under its own power

- A speed limit of 80km/h in practice and 120km/h during the warm-up and race, or such other speed limits as the F1 Commission may decide, will be enforced in the pit lane.
- Any driver who exceeds the pit lane speed limit will be fined US$250 for each km/h above the limit (this may be increased for a second offence in the same season). During the race the stewards may impose a time penalty on any driver who exceeds the limit.
- The car's rear light must be illuminated whenever it is running on wet tyres. No penalty will be imposed if the light fails during a race, nor does the car need to stop.
- If a car stops during practice it must be removed from the track as soon as possible. If the driver is unable to drive the car from a dangerous position, it is the duty of marshals to assist him. If such assistance results in the car being pushed back to the pits, the car may not be used again during that session. If the assistance is given during a qualifying period, the driver's fastest time from the relevant session will be deleted.
- If, in the opinion of stewards, a stoppage is caused deliberately, the driver concerned may have his times from that session cancelled and may not be permitted to take part in any other practice session that day.
- The grid will be a staggered 1 x 1 formation with each car separated by 8 metres.

The race weekend

On track action gets underway at 11am Friday morning, a good time to see the cars out on the circuit.

For hard working truckies, a Grand Prix meeting starts as early as Tuesday before the race when they arrive with the team's articulated trucks and start to set up the garage.

The race teams and media contingent generally start to arrive on Thursday — a day earlier at Monte Carlo — and drivers are selected at random for an FIA press conference on Thursday and Friday afternoons.

Supersoft qualifying tyres are a thing of the past

Such has been the explosion of interest in Grand Prix racing that attendance at press conferences is mandatory for drivers, with heavy fines imposed for a no-show. Also, any driver who finishes in the championship top three and absents himself from the end-of-season FIA prize giving earns himself a $50,000 fine!

Scrutineering takes place on Thursday and the cars first take to the track at 11:00am on Friday for one hour. There is a break of one hour before the second session of free practice between 1.00 and 2.00 pm.

Saturday's second session of free practice is an earlier start, with cars on track between 9.00 and 9.45 and then 10.15 and 11.00. A two hour break follows before the all-important

Such has been the explosion of interest in Grand Prix racing that attendance at press conferences is mandatory (see below).

qualifying hour at 13.00.

The teams are permitted to use two different tyre compounds on Friday and Saturday morning. Before qualifying, however, they must decide on which compound they want to select for qualifying and the race. These are then marked by a member of the FIA technical staff and represent a driver's complete allocation for the rest of the meeting.

Supersoft qualifying tyres worth multiple seconds and good for just one lap are thus an expensive feature of the past. Even so, a new set of rubber might be worth half to three quarters of a second per lap depending on the circuit. Drivers are allowed a maximum of 12 qualifying laps and so they tend to mount four separate three-lap attacks on qualifying. The first is an 'out' lap used to bring the tyres up to temperature, the second is the 'hot' lap and the third an 'in' lap.

It has been known for drivers/teams to miscount the number of laps completed. If this happens, all of a competitor's qualifying laps are deleted and he must start the race from the back of the grid.

In order to start the race, a driver must qualify within 107 per cent of the pole position time. Exceptions to this can be made in special circumstances, for instance if a car breaks, there is no spare available to the driver and he has already shown himself capable of setting a qualifying time in an earlier session. This decision is at the FIA's discretion.

For the drivers and teams, Friday and Saturday are spent refamiliarising themselves with the circuit and testing the wear characteristics of tyres at various fuel loads and temperatures. Whenever possible a team will

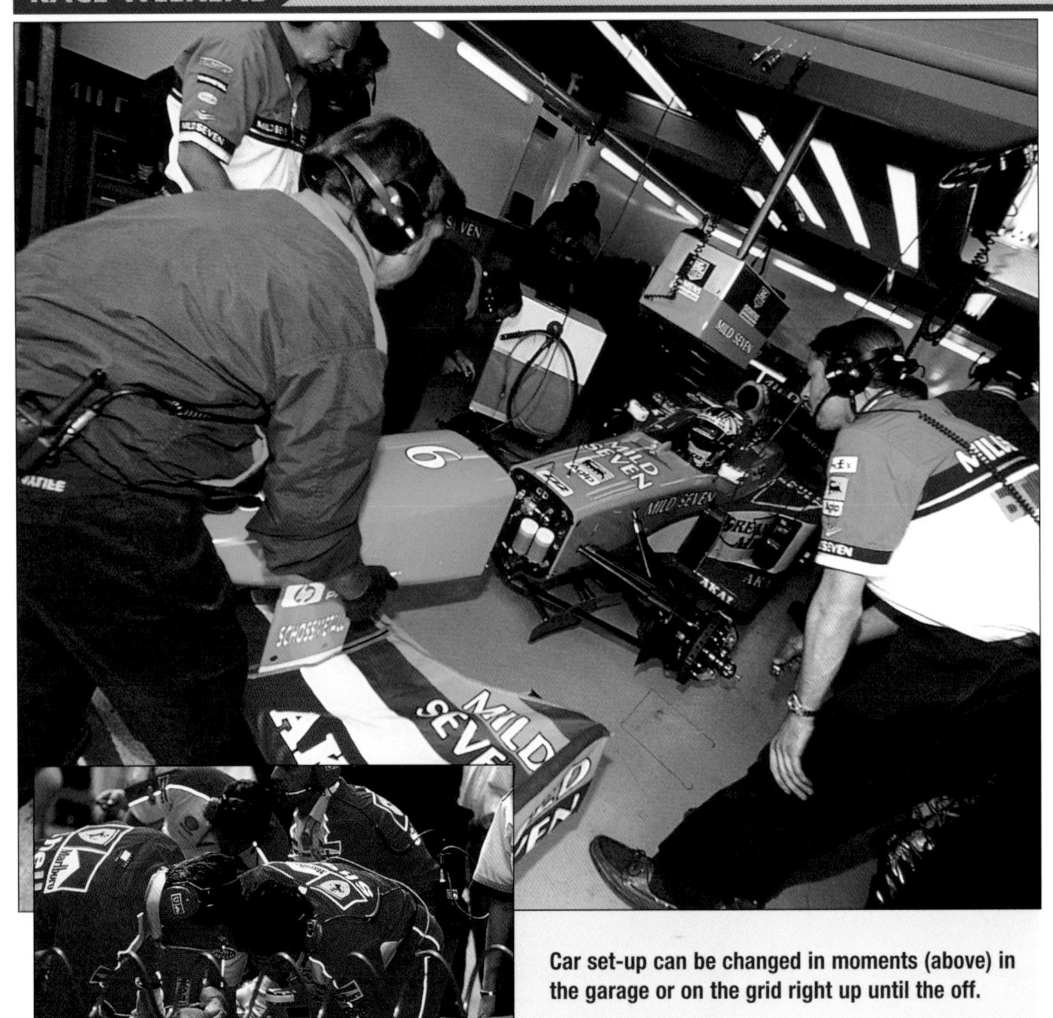

Car set-up can be changed in moments (above) in the garage or on the grid right up until the off.

choose the softer of the two available tyre compounds provided that the wear characteristics do not look marginal for the race.

For spectators keen to investigate the circuit and possibly photograph the cars in action, Friday and Saturday morning are the times to do it. Friday especially. There is no longer a restriction on the number of laps which cars may run in free practice, so there is considerable activity. Also, the qualifying hour is deserving of full attention as one of the most spectacular periods of the entire race weekend.

Qualifying makes for spectacular viewing

Because the drivers are at the limit, especially on their third and fourth runs if a 'banker' time is already established, qualifying makes for spectacular viewing. While nothing can beat standing on the outside of somewhere like Casino Square in Monte Carlo at such a time, so good is the TV coverage of racing these days that the drama of the session perhaps unfolds best in front of a TV screen.

Split times around the lap give clues as to the ultimate potential of the lap and the tension mounts as the 60 minutes draw to a close. Action in the first 20 minutes can be sparse as nobody wants to go out and clean the track for the rest. This is especially true at dusty venues like Hungaroring. Inevitably, it seems, a Minardi will venture out to gain some screen time for its sponsors!

The public relations role is an integral part of a driver's duties.

One way to have the best of both worlds — the action and the information — is to place yourself near one of the huge spectator screens around the circuit and hope that the sun is not too strong.

Once grid positions are decided, teams will strip down chassis, install fresh engines for the race and pore over the telemetry data accumulated during the day. Driver/engineer debriefs can stretch well into the evening and it can be an especially long night for the bolters (mechanics).

On Saturday evening a driver may be required to attend a sponsor function or dinner once he has finished at the circuit, although most teams prefer to get these commitments over on a Thursday or Friday. The driver's task does not finish there, however. Often he will visit the Paddock Club after the race morning warm-up and briefing, where he might give privileged sponsor guests an insight into the race they are about to see and answer a few questions. Then it's back to the team motorhome for some specially prepared food and perhaps an hour to collect himself before the big race.

Detailed scrutineering checks take place the day before a Grand Prix meeting starts.

The race

The start of a Grand Prix is perhaps the most spectacular sight in world sport. Twenty-two cars unleash approximately 17,500 horsepower in a technicolour blur and cacophony of noise. It has to be experienced to be believed.

The start is often critical to the outcome. Overtaking is notoriously difficult in modern F1 because cars lose front wing efficiency when running close to one another. That promotes understeer (the front end wants to go straight on) which makes it difficult for a driver to follow closely enough onto a straight to be able to launch an outbraking bid at the end of it. The problem is exacerbated by the efficiency of F1's carbon brakes, which make braking distances, and hence outbraking opportunities, so short.

While a Grand Prix used to start when the red lights changed to green, a new procedure now involves five red lights systematically going out, to the point where the race begins when the last one is extinguished. The grid contains sensors at the position where the cars line up and a special transponder on the car triggers a warning if the driver jumps the start. A 10 second stop-go penalty in the pits is the reward.

Once the race is underway, tactics come into play. Teams use computer simulations to arrive at the optimum number of pit stops to employ

Grid positions are the result of two days' intense effort. A race start with 17,500bhp on tap is an awesome spectacle and the first few yards can be decisive.

Fuelling takes longer than bolting on fresh rubber and dictates the length of a pit stop.

during a race. This will vary depending on many factors. Foremost among them is the car's grid position. It is no good deciding that the quickest way is to run a light fuel load and stop three times if the car is on the third row of the grid. Lighter fuel loads may enable

Red alert – the ins and outs of an F1 pi

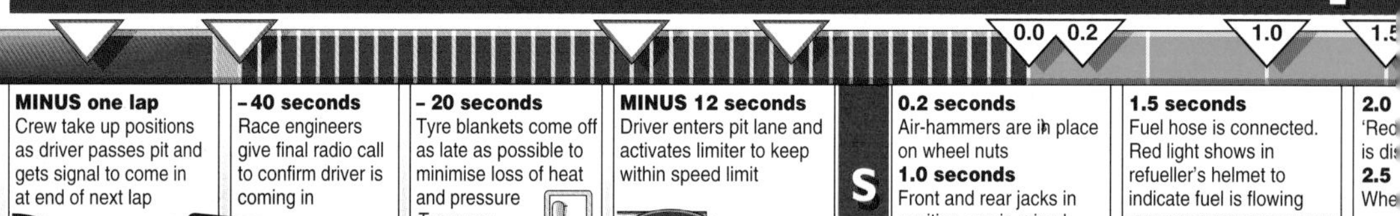

MINUS one lap
Crew take up positions as driver passes pit and gets signal to come in at end of next lap

- 40 seconds
Race engineers give final radio call to confirm driver is coming in

- 20 seconds
Tyre blankets come off as late as possible to minimise loss of heat and pressure
Tyres are pre-heated to around 90ßC

MINUS 12 seconds
Driver enters pit lane and activates limiter to keep within speed limit

0.2 seconds
Air-hammers are in place on wheel nuts
1.0 seconds
Front and rear jacks in position, car is raised

1.5 seconds
Fuel hose is connected. Red light shows in refueller's helmet to indicate fuel is flowing

2.0
'Red
is di
2.5
Whe

1. **Rear jack:** follows car in, raises rear end
2. **Wheel off:** removes used wheels *(man on left rear then moves to take up position at rear of car, standing by with starter)*
3. **Hammer:** removes and fixes wheel nuts
4. **Wheel on:** positions new wheel
5. **Refueller:** delivers pre-set fuel load
6. **Hose support:** steadies hose during refuelling
7. **Balance:** holds car steady while on jacks
8. **Rig minder:** operates 'dead-man's handle' *(cuts fuel flow in emergency)*
9. **Brake board:** gives driver instructions
10. **Front jack:** raises front end of car
11. **Visor wipe:** cleans driver's helmet visor

A smoking getaway, but strict pit lane speed limits are in force.

the car to lap more quickly, but not if it is stuck behind a heavier car making fewer stops. It may be the optimum strategy if the car is on pole, however, or, as in Hungary last year with Michael Schumacher, if the driver is able to make up an inordinate

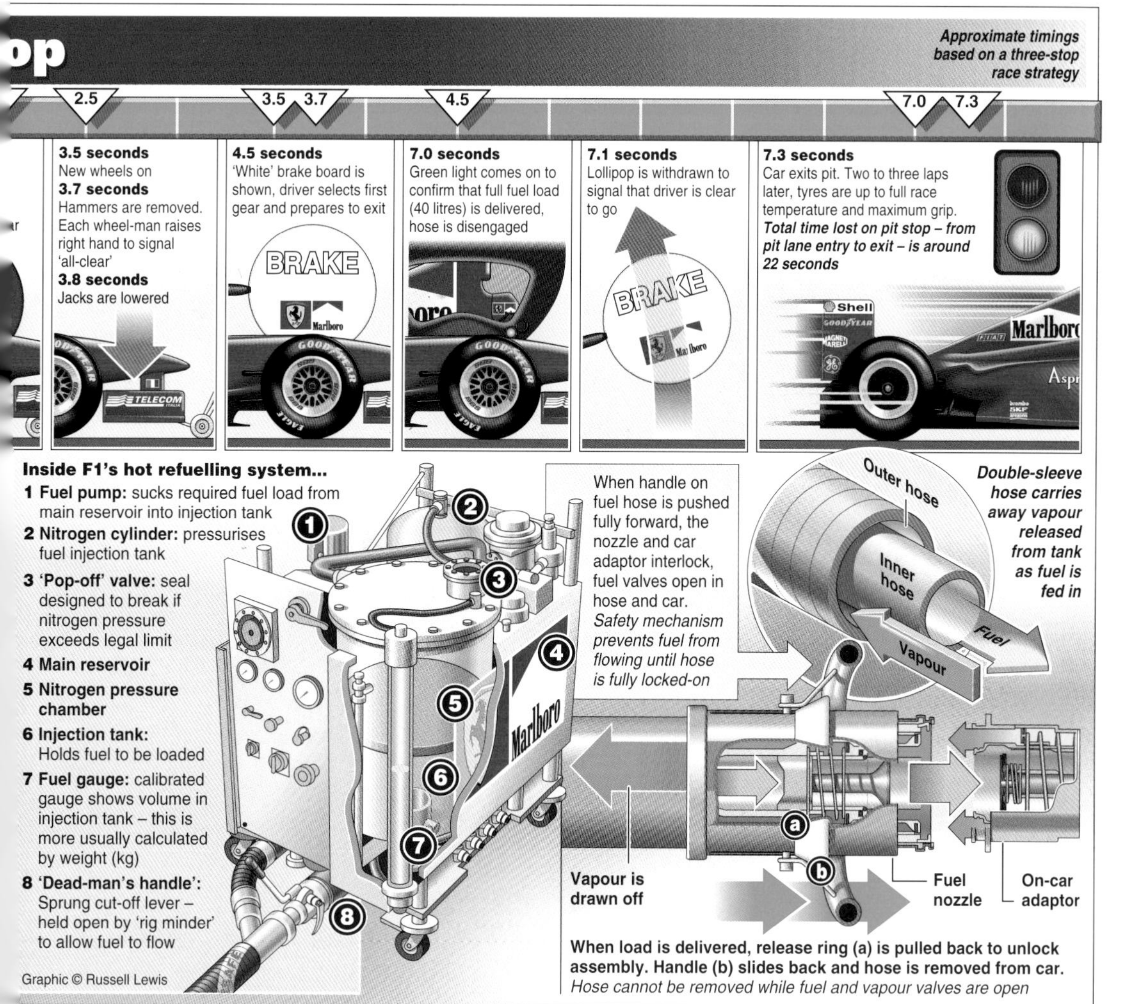

The braking capability of a modern F1 car is phenomenal. Braking distances are short, overtaking difficult and team strategy vital.

Refuelling was reintroduced in 1994. A well-drilled crew can make all the difference.

amount of time during a mid-race stint.

Knowing that they will be making a pit stop to refuel, many drivers will hope to gain positions by stopping at the right time rather than by chancing risky overtaking moves. There is an undoubted art to driving superfast 'in' and 'out' laps without ignominious collisions with the pit wall.

Drivers will hope to gain positions by stopping at the right time

The time taken by the stop itself is dictated by refuelling. The pit crews are so well drilled that four tyres can be changed in around five seconds, leaving the fuel flow (around 10 litres per second) as the decisive factor.

Mika Hakkinen's consistent speed on fresh rubber after his first pit stop was key to his crucial win at Nurburgring last year.

So much for the time taken, but the timing is also crucial. A driver returning to the race may be on a heavier fuel load but he will also have the benefit of fresh tyres. If he pushes as hard as possible, he may be able to overhaul a driver who was ahead of him but waits longer before his stop. A common Schumacher tactic, Mika Hakkinen turned the tables on the Ferrari driver in this way at Nurburgring last year to score a decisive win and set up his championship success at Suzuka.

Technology

The 1992 season was a defining moment for Grand Prix racing. Williams had perfected active suspension, whereby computer controlled ride height optimised the car's aerodynamics. Nelson Piquet had run an active Williams at Monza six years earlier but development was slow. Ironically, Nigel Mansell had been a strong critic after suffering a couple of frights during the 1988 season.

In '92, however, Mansell was the benefactor, storming to his first world championship. He won the first five races of the season and had the championship sewn up by Hungaroring in August. In the first race, at Kyalami, a disgruntled reigning champion Ayrton Senna finished 35 seconds behind. 'In equal equipment,' he said, 'it just doesn't happen like that...'

It was Max Mosley's first full season in control at the FIA. At first he said he was committed to allowing Formula 1 to follow its technological course, but later admitted that he hadn't fully

Every so often a car redefines performance levels. Nigel Mansell's 1992 Williams did just that. Below: Analysing data in the pits.

understood exactly how far things had gone. At Spa that year, Mansell himself said: 'Once we drop the clutch, the computer and the software will decide who has the best traction off the line.'

The art of gear-changing had been taken away and now the start was governed by electronics. Things were going too far. Four wheel steering was on the way and when McLaren launched the MP4/8 for 1993, team boss Ron Dennis acclaimed it as the most sophisticated racing car of all time. It would not be too long, he said, before a car could do a lap of its own accord, sensing where it was on the circuit and acting accordingly.

It would not be long before a car could lap on its own

Undeniably, the driver's contribution was gradually being eroded. While there was support for taking things back to basics, the idea was obviously unpopular with teams such as McLaren and Williams who had invested enormous sums in mastering the technology. Unsurprisingly the FIA could not achieve the necessary unanimous agreement for a ban on driver aids and had to act in a more heavy-handed way.

At Montreal in 1993 a bulletin from technical delegate Charlie Whiting declared that everyone except Minardi was illegal. Their active systems contravened a rule precluding moveable aerodynamic devices, and traction control was unlawful because the rules said that drivers needed to be in control of their cars at all times.

Technology peaked in 1993 (above) but still had frightening consequences for Karl Wendlinger a year later (below). Following his crash at Monaco cockpit head padding became mandatory.

The FIA pointed out that it was perfectly within its rights to demand that everyone turn up in France without active suspension a couple of weeks later. However, if the major players could see their way to agreeing a driver aids ban for 1994, that would suffice... They added that they could cancel all the control systems on safety grounds if they so desired.

The governing body's case was strengthened when Alessandro Zanardi suffered a Lotus active failure at Spa's daunting Eau Rouge.

'I don't remember a lot,' Zanardi said, 'but we had a yellow light in the car which came on if you had a pressure failure in the active system. I just had time to see the warning light come on and think: "Oh God, not here..."

At the same time, Benetton was experimenting with an auto start system which, said some, had a laser which sensed the change in current between the red and green light at the start of a race and kicked in the auto start. The team denied it but such talk was reflective of the time. Things had gone too far.

For 1994, then, a ban on driver aids was pushed through. Active suspension, traction control, four wheel steering — all were gone. Semi-automatic gearboxes stayed because they eliminated the damage caused when drivers over-revved on a downchange and thus saved a fortune in engine bills.

Some thought that the ban should have been extended to include telemetry. On board sensors recording a car's every move produced reams of data which the teams and drivers could mull over at their leisure. Drivers within the same team could see where a team mate was later on the brakes, earlier on the power or myriad other

Benetton's wheel of fortune

Since the 'paddle' gear-shift mechanism first appeared on the steering wheel of a sceptical Nigel Mansell's Ferrari in Brazil, 1989, an inestimable amount of time and money has been invested in turning one of the car's most basic components into a major nerve-centre.
Today's drivers have both hands firmly fixed to a technological masterpiece that is worth rather more than its weight in gold!

So what are all those flashing lights and buttons about? Read on as all is revealed...

Traffic signals: lights set in top of steering wheel give a constant guide to car's running status

'SL' (Gear shift): sequential lights pre-set to specific 'rev' bands – determined by individual circuit characteristics and conditions – tell drivers when to change gear

A/D:	Spare
B/C:	**Pit lane speed limiter on**
E:	Radio indicator
F/H:	**Clutch (separate left and right paddle indicators)**
G:	Throttle. Pre-sets allow indication of optimum throttle level for start
J:	**Second pit limiter indicator**

Reverse gear: on the back of the steering wheel...

1: Gear up-shift
2: Gear down-shift
3/4: Clutch paddles

The right connections: wheel 'plugs in' to the car via a set of pins that lock into corresponding sockets on the tip of the steering column

Function mode (-): works in conjuction with main function selector switch, button scrolls ***down*** through setting options. '(+)' button scrolls ***up***

Function mode (+)

'Flag' lights *(experimental)*

Spare

E48 16000 266
6 1:26:32 86°

PO
P1 IGN
P2
SCROLL
OFF
LIGHT
ON
REVERSE

Radio button

Neutral selector

Pit lane limiter button

Main function selector

FAIL DISP THR BRK RS BAL 5 6 7 8 9 10
MAP
MIX

Two-way engine map group switch: allows instant switching of engine maps when car is in pits

Fuel mix : five-way switch allows fuel mixture to be modified on-track

Logger switch: Should a problem occur on-track, button can 'mark' telemetry read-out for later analysis by engineers

Main function switch: determines which data is displayed on screen and activates selected programme

DISP: scrolls display of pressure data on various circuits such as compressed air and brakes

FAIL: simulates selected component failure – used for testing only!

BAL: sets front-to-rear brake balance (15 settings)

FAIL DISP THR BRK RS BAL 10
Reserve channels

Engine data and settings

THR: controls throttle function to Mecachrome specifications (5 settings)

BRK: controls engine braking effect to preserve rear brakes (5 settings)

RS: spare channel for Mechachrome settings

Screen display: a massive range of data can be displayed on integral screen. Illustration below represents a 'typical' on-track display

Error ID: if a fault develops on-track, driver can radio number to engineers. Using this code, the team can indentify the problem and tell the driver if it is safe to continue or if he must pit

Engine revs
Speed (km/h)

E48 16000 266
6 1:26:32 86°

Gear
Lap time – *display will flash to indicate a best time*
Water temp.

Discovery of auto start software in Benetton's computer programme tarnished Michael Schumacher's first championship win in 1994.

factors. They could take the data back to their hotel, mull it over and come back next day for another go. Gerhard Berger, for one, thought it took away a substantial part of natural seat-of-the-pants driving.

The other concern was the possibility of teams making changes to their cars while racing was in progress, outside a driver's control. Or even, whisper it, making changes to the opposition's cars. A rule was introduced allowing only car to pit data transmission. A team could thereby still receive due warning if a car failure was imminent.

The problem, of course, is that you cannot uninvent technology. Once software expertise exists, who can tell whether a team is employing it? The result was an atmosphere of suspicion in the paddock as the decade developed. Michael Schumacher's first championship win with Benetton in 1994 was tarnished by constant paddock suspicion and innuendo after the FIA discovered auto start (launch control) software in the team's computer programme. The Benetton defence, and they were not alone, said that it was easier to disable banned systems than to rewrite software programmes and risk introducing errors.

The problem is that you cannot uninvent technology

Much of the controversy as the decade unfolded surrounded attempts to effectively duplicate traction control in all but name. This could be achieved through complex throttle mapping techniques. McLaren also tried an ingenious second brake system which was banned in controversial circumstances at the 1998 Brazilian Grand Prix. The fight is a constant one: the governing body attempting to sustain a level playing field against brilliant technical brains with mega-buck funding.

The start of the 1998 season brought narrower track cars and grooved tyres in an attempt to cap lap speeds.

What does it all cost?

Some of the British constructors are fond of claiming that Ferrari, given its budget, should win every race. True enough, the Italian team is estimated to have spent £100 million in 1998.

Approximately 20 per cent of that went on one man: Michael Schumacher. Ferrari, though, is the exception. What they paid Schumacher actually exceeded Minardi's entire operating budget!

Williams, with 'Sir Frank' and pragmatic engineering partner Patrick Head controlling the purse strings, is probably a better example. For them, the biggest single expense of 1998 was engines, unusual for a team which enjoyed

Sponsors spend substantial amounts of money on circuit advertising as well as on the cars.

works backing from Renault for the previous nine years.

It is virtually impossible to compete without a major manufacturer as a technical partner. Honda dominated with McLaren, poured in millions and then stopped. Today, Mercedes is thought to spend at least £30 million each year on its investment in McLaren.

Suddenly, Williams and Benetton, after enjoying Renault works support, were faced with £12 million bills for Mecachrome engine lease deals. The same situation applies in 1999 when the teams share the engine (now named Supertec) with newly-formed British American Racing.

How can it be so expensive? Well, consider that Renault Sport had a staff of over 150 to build its engines. There were 28 engineers, 20 draughtsmen, 35 mechanics, eight electronics specialists, 20 machinists and fitters, four systems engineers, six bench technicians, 15 in purchase, production and quality control and

Twenty million pounds a year, but is he happy? You bet! Michael Schumacher is top money earner.

another 15 administrative staff. With the race schedule, spare car, and a separate test team always on the go, each team needed around 40 engines. For Williams, BMW's arrival in 2000 no doubt cannot come soon enough!

Although 1998 was a poor year by Williams standards, the team would have spent an estimated £10 million in the research and development phase of producing the car. And McLaren, probably, more. At the launch of the championship winning MP4-13, team boss Ron Dennis explained that the car 'was a consequence of 12,000 man hours of aerodynamic development'.

Teams such as Williams and Benetton employ 300 people. Costing the average salary at

Watching in style. Corporate hospitality is an integral part of the F1 scene.

£20,000, which is conservative, the team's annual wage bill adds up to more than £6 million. Informed sources suggest that as reigning world champion, Jacques Villeneuve commanded a similar amount, with Heinz-Harald Frentzen on nearer £4 million. Add in operating costs of another £16 million and the team's budget is not far short of £60 million.

As far as driver earnings go, there is Schumacher and then the rest. Like Senna before him, Schumacher is viewed as a man who can make the difference and is paid accordingly. Behind him, drivers like Villeneuve and Hakkinen command an estimated £6 million, with established aces like Frentzen, Damon Hill, David Coulthard, Jean Alesi and Johnny Herbert also on multi million pound retainers. Arguably, though, driver salaries have actually declined during the nineties.

Bernie Ecclestone always used to quote the lightbulb theory when it came to paying his drivers. Tongue only partially in cheek, he would argue that you simply unplug one and plug in his replacement. Unless you have the very best of the time — and today it's Schumacher — there is merit in the argument. With a reduction in the number of cars (22) for the same driver pool, it is also more of a

Commercial sponsorship first appeared in the late sixties.

buyer's market for the teams.

The simple business realities of F1 lead to the Pay Driver — an anomaly in a sport which prides itself on excellence. Arrows is a good example. In 1997 Tom Walkinshaw spent an estimated £4.5 million to secure Damon Hill. Pedro Diniz, meanwhile, is believed to have paid around £7 million for each of his two years with the team.

There are pay drivers and pay drivers. Diniz's problem is that he will never be taken entirely seriously as a driver, despite being far better than perceived. Nobody, however, views Rubens Barrichello as a pay driver. And yet Stewart is believed to have benefited to the tune of £4 million from the Brazilian's personal backers. Out of that, Barrichello will be on an estimated £1.5 – 2 million.

Cigarette money pays most of the F1 bills

Although Stewart's engine supplier, Ford, prefers a policy of non-tobacco association, it is cigarette money which pays most of the F1 bills. The Marlboro, West, Winfield, Mild Seven, Benson & Hedges, Gauloises and now Lucky Strike and 555 brands (through British American Tobacco) are all title sponsors of big budget F1 teams. Mild Seven also supports Minardi, while Sauber has a title sponsorship deal with Malaysian petrol company Petronas. That leaves Arrows as the only other F1 team without major tobacco investors.

The money involved is colossal. At the announcement of British American Racing, there was talk of a £300 million investment over five years. That is even more than Marlboro contributes for its presence on the Ferraris, estimated at £50 million in 1998.

The simple fact is that with so many advertising restrictions on tobacco, F1 cars are a fantastic advertising medium for cigarette companies. If it weren't so, they wouldn't pay.

As well as identification on cars, sponsors also spend substantial amounts on circuit advertising and corporate hospitality. At each Grand Prix there are around 40 large advertising hoardings, sold for around £60,000 each. Allsport Management boss Paddy NcNally is responsible for them and has also developed the exclusive Paddock Club hospitality facility into another strong revenue source, estimated to produce £25 million a year. It is often used as a business tool: corporate high flyers are entertained in champagne style at a cost of up to £2000 a head over the three days of a Grand Prix meeting.